WHAT PEOPLE
ARE SAYING ABOUT

THE RFACTOR

"The *RFactor offers innovative insights into succeeding in business and beyond with universal relationship rhythms.*"

- Dr. Greg Reid,
Award-winning speaker and author of
28 bestsellers, including *Three Feet from Gold*
and his most recent title, *Wealth Made Easy*

"*The challenges and rewards of nurturing prosperous relationships begin within each of us. From mindset to life lessons, Ashby and Segal creatively coach the reader to view their own lives through the story of two characters.*"

- David Corbin,
Mentor to mentors,
four-time *Wall Street Journal* bestselling author,
two-time international award-winning inventor

"Whether you're an entrepreneur, solopreneur, C-Suite executive, a student of life and looking for love, or newly entering the workforce, The RFactor is the book for you. Through storytelling, the authors artfully shine a beacon on the power of connected relationships and take the reader on a journey of self-discovery. It's AWESOME!"

- Erik Swanson,
13-time #1 international bestselling author, Founder of Habitude Warrior and Speaker Hearts, award-winning TEDx featured speaker, and creator of AuthorResource.com

"This book is filled with transformational leadership nuggets. It will serve corporate teams, individuals, executives, entrepreneurs, young adults, and families throughout their personal and professional lives. It's worth having on every desk as a tool to return to regularly."

- Dr. Judith Rich,
Pioneering teacher and thought leader in the field of leadership transformation and consciousness, bestselling author of *Beyond the Box*

"Ashby and Segal have brought a fresh perspective to exploring the power of mastering connected relationships both personally and professionally. As master leaders themselves, living and working together, they are a great example of head and heart leadership."

- Michael Strasner,
Visionary, Corporate Trainer, Mentor and Coach, Amazon #1 Best Selling Author, *Living on The Skinny Branches*, *Mastering Leadership: Shift the Drift and Change The World*

DISCOVER the UNIVERSAL RHYTHMS for
LEADING PROSPEROUS RELATIONSHIPS

THE **R** FACTOR

E V O L V I N G

OUR HUMAN RELATIONSHIP STORY

KEN ASHBY

MARIS SEGAL

The *R*Factor

Discover the Universal Rhythms
for Leading Prosperous Relationships

Ken Ashby and Maris Segal

Copyright © 2023
ISBN: 979-8-9859524-2-1

Joint Venture Publishing, Blue Sky

JOINT VENTURE
PUBLISHING

For quantity discounts or bulk purchases,
contact www.SegalLeadershipGlobal.com

DEDICATION

We dedicate this book to our parents, who were connected in life and love, each married over fifty years. Their spirit and energy continue to inspire our relationships every day.

They modeled for us how to show respect, be responsible, reframe limiting beliefs, and stand up with resilience.
We are their living legacy.
Robert and Debra Segal
John and Jean Ashby

And to our beautiful family for whom
we stand in gratitude every day…
Kim and Jett
Cindy, Grace, Sam, and Will
Ryan and Amanda
John, Adriana, Kaylee, Peyton, and Blayke

We honor our relationships with each of you and look forward to all the adventures that will continue to unfold.

THE RFACTOR

1

CONNECTION

Relationships begin with a connection,
and the one relationship that you can't leave home
without is ... YOU.

A smile lit up Mindi's face as the band finished their last number in the long-awaited and highly-publicized last tour of one of the biggest bands in the last two decades. Now 38, Mindi had been just a teen when the band got its start and quickly climbed the charts as they became one of the most popular groups connecting generations, from teens to adults. The fact that they had broken into the top of the charts with their first hit song was impressive. Even more impressive, though, was the fact that the band's popularity hadn't waned since then; in fact, they had just hit another #1. As Mindi had just witnessed, every concert, including this one in LA, usually sold out within hours after tickets became available, and the standing-room-only crowd at the arena tonight was no different. Hearing the cheering full-house crowd, Mindi was grateful for another concert that had gone off without a glitch.

It was nights like these that made Mindi love her work. As an executive concert producer in the music business, she had a reputation for being one of the top concert producers in the country, a recognition that she'd held with great appreciation and respect for nearly a decade. Professional musicians were always happy to perform when she was the producer at a venue because they knew everything would go smoothly. Under Mindi's supervision and leadership, no details were overlooked and there weren't any surprises. She knew her audiences, and she did her homework, always knowing beforehand all of the significant and even minor details that impressed those she served, whether it was on stage or behind the scenes. Her attention to detail was unsurpassed in the music industry, with attention not only to the artists that performed, but also their production, business, marketing, and management teams.

Most people thought she had a dream job, and she was no exception. Who wouldn't love to rub shoulders with platinum-award-winning artists and have access to everyone in their circle? To some, she was the definition of lucky; to Mindi, though, her success was the product of hard work, learning, research, and, most important, connected, trusted, professional relationships that had taken years to build.

The band had finished their encore, and the road crew had started taking down the lights and sound equipment and would soon begin packing the road cases and loading multiple semi-trucks. Mindi was making her post-concert rounds. Satisfied that the crowd had dispersed and the front-of-house details were all in good order, she exited the hall and started to return to the backstage area, where she would have her first opportunity to breathe, have a quick bite, and spend a little time with her favorite childhood band, who were now close and who counted on Mindi to run a tight ship.

As she rounded the corner, she was caught by surprise when she ran into a tall man with dark hair that had the slightest sprinkle of gray at the temples. Not one to forget a face, Mindi knew right away that she had never met the man and wondered how he'd gotten past security.

"Can I help you?" she asked in her most professional voice that was softened by a sunny smile.

"Um, maybe," the man stammered, trying to figure out why the attractive blonde woman before him looked familiar. "Hey, wait! Aren't you Mindi Rhodes—the Mindi Rhodes who produces some of the biggest concerts in the music industry?"

"Yes, I am. What can I do for you?" she asked.

"Wow. It's a privilege to meet you! You don't know me—*yet*. I'm Rich … Rich Holmes." Following his introduction, he handed her one of his signature business cards—a clear business card with a QR code that linked to a secure web page, which contained his contact information and a catalogue of the songs he'd written.

"Hello, Rich," Mindi replied before her recall kicked in. "Wait a minute—I've seen this card before!"

"You have? Well, that's pretty awesome, but I don't believe we've met before so..."

"No, we haven't, but I had the pleasure of having lunch last week with a couple of colleagues who are publishers and agents," Mindi explained. "As a matter of fact, I was sitting across from them when one pulled your QR card out, and we all listened to one of your songs. Hmmm, what was the name of that song? It was pretty good. I do remember that. But mostly, I remember your card. It's unforgettable, actually. What a creative and convenient way to give people access to your music!"

"Thank you, Mindi. You don't know how much that means to me. I have written a couple songs that have been published, but I'm still looking to write that one song that'll make all the difference in my career. As a matter of fact, I think I'm close," he said. "If you get a chance, I'd love for you to listen to it. It's the most recent song uploaded to my catalogue."

"I'll do that, Rich," Mindi replied. "But right now, I have to get back to work. Were you looking for someone or..."

"I was actually hoping I would come across a member of the crew or someone who could get my card to Silver Daughter or their manager. But running into you is even better!" he exclaimed.

"Well, I'm not sure about that," Mindi quipped.

The music business is known for its exclusivity, and managers, agents, publishers, and artists intentionally make it difficult for songwriters and fans to have access to them. While the separation was intended to protect those professionals, it made it extremely difficult for unpublished songwriters and indie artists to get noticed. Mindi knew the protocol very well, and she had worked very hard to make sure she was trusted in the business. Part of building and maintaining that industry trust meant that she couldn't encourage strangers who might be trying to use her to get close to musicians, something which she'd always been very cognizant of throughout the years. But there was something about Rich that told her he was being on the up-and-up. The next words out of her mouth were unprecedented, and they came as a surprise, even to her.

"You know what?" the petite blonde answered. "You've gone to all the trouble to try to get a backdoor introduction, do you want to come backstage with me?"

"That'd be great! But I don't want to intrude or anything," he said, knowing she was going out on a limb by extending the invitation.

"Well, I like your ingenuity, and I figured that anyone who would take the risk of getting kicked out by security and setting themselves up to inconveniently run into me must be pretty dedicated. At the very least, you managed to get past security, and in my book, that's impressive. It's fine, and you're not intruding, especially since you are known by a couple of my friends in the industry," she said.

"Oh, I promise I am harmless!" Rich replied eagerly.

"Well, then, what do you say about meeting the band?" she smiled.

"Who? Me? You're inviting me backstage *to meet the band*?!"

"That's what I said," she grinned again at his excitement. "This business is all about relationships, and if you really want to break into it, it definitely helps to know someone. Now you can say you know me, Rich. You never know, it might be the start of something. But I'm not making any promises."

"No promises. I get it," Rich declared. "But every introduction is an opportunity, isn't it? And it looks like I just stumbled into one!"

Laughing, she replied.

"Well, I'm not so sure we stumbled. I'd like to think it was more graceful than that," Mindi pointed out. "Come on, we better get moving if you want to meet the band before they leave."

Inspired by her energy and enthusiasm, Rich followed her down the hall, grateful for their chance encounter. He had just met the woman who was going to let him meet the band. He had no idea where it would take him, but like every song he'd ever written, he hoped it would be the first verse in what might ultimately seal his place as a professional songwriter. He'd always wanted to write that one song that would open a door to his notoriety, and he dared to hope that this night would be that connection.

2

OPPORTUNITY

We are where we are when we're meant to be.

It wasn't the first time Rich had been backstage after a performance, but it was the most memorable invitation he'd accepted. For one thing, the band, Silver Daughter, was one of the biggest names in the business, and an opportunity to meet its members was without a doubt an invitation that few, if any, would turn down. For super fans, it would be a dream come true. For a songwriter like Rich, it meant being invited into an exclusive, tight-knit circle that could open doors to the fame he'd longed for since the day he'd penned his first song many years before.

From the moment he walked through the door, Mindi made sure he felt comfortable. Whether she was introducing him to the drummer or letting the bodyguards know he was her guest and, therefore, welcome in the room, she went out of her way to make sure he didn't feel out of place. It was obvious to Rich that she was well respected and liked by everyone, but it didn't escape his attention that while she had earned their trust, she never let her guard down. She was constantly on the lookout for anything amiss. It wouldn't be the first time she'd have to cut off someone who was overserved or rescue an artist who couldn't get away from an admiring fan.

As soon as Mindi saw the first sign that the band was ready to wrap it up, she subtly directed to the bartender that it was last call and asked the caterer to start taking down the food tables. Rich watched from the sidelines as she walked through the room and thanked them for their service.

Taking the cue, Rich approached her to say goodbye and thank her for her hospitality.

"Give me a minute to grab my things," she said, "and I'll walk out with you."

As they exited the arena, she indicated she was parked close by and could give him a ride to his car—an invitation he gladly accepted.

"So, I bet you're ready to go home and put your feet up," he commented.

"Well, I should, but I'm starving. I usually get a bite to eat before heading home," she said. "There's an all-night pancake house down the street that I often go to," and before she realized it, she heard herself say, "Do you want to join me?"

Surprised by the offer, Rich said, "Sure, I'd like that," welcoming the opportunity to get to know her a little better.

Ten minutes later, they were seated and had already placed their orders.

"An omelet, hash browns, and toast," Rich said as he lifted his coffee cup. "I'm guessing you don't eat much on days like today."

"Yeah, like most concert days, I got to work at 10:00 this morning, and I barely remember eating a sandwich on the run," she sighed.

"A 14-hour day, huh? You must be exhausted," he said.

"I'm used to it," she said, shrugging her shoulders. "It is a long day, but it takes a large team and a lot of preparation and coordination to put on a concert of this caliber. We work to exceed the expectations of the musicians and make sure the audience gets the show they deserve."

"Well, judging by what I experienced tonight, it seemed flawless," he complimented her.

"Thank you," she laughed.

"Tell me, how did you get into producing concerts?" Rich asked.

"I kind of fell into it. When I graduated from college, I got an internship and was introduced to someone who took me under his wing and mentored me. After a couple years working alongside him, I became his assistant, and he taught me everything he knew. Funny, I wasn't even looking for a career in the music industry, but here I am."

"What do you like the most about your job?" he asked.

"The money and, on most days, the people," she answered without hesitating.

"Most people would give anything to get to be on a first-name basis with the artists and groups you work with," he agreed.

"I'm sure, and the fact that I'm fortunate isn't lost on me, but the job isn't all about rubbing shoulders with the rich and famous," she corrected.

"Oh?" he asked, pushing her to elaborate. "What don't you like about it?"

"For starters, there is a lot of pressure and little room for error, and I work nearly every weekend, which is not conducive to a family life, let alone a social life. I have a six-year-old at home, and if it wasn't for my parents, I couldn't do it."

"No husband?" asked Rich.

"No. My daughter's father isn't very involved, so I count on my parents to take care of Rose when I'm working." Mindi replied.

"You must have a staff, people who take some of your work off your plate, so you don't have to put in so many hours on days like today?" he inquired.

"Don't get me wrong—I have a great team, but ultimately, the responsibility for producing concerts of this magnitude falls on me. It's what I signed up for, and I take my job seriously, which means that I can't rely on anyone else to make sure everything goes smoothly."

Then turning the conversation toward him, Mindi felt comfortable enough to ask, "How about you, Rich? Are you married? Do you have kids?"

"No to both," he answered nonchalantly as he took a sip of his coffee.

"Oh, are you a perpetual bachelor?" she teased. "Determined that you'll never settle down?"

"It probably looks that way," he chuckled, "but I guess I just never met the right person at the right time. I'm married to my work all week as a stockbroker, and I've enjoyed a great deal of success over the years. I'm fortunate that I'm in a position financially that I can step back when I want, or even retire altogether. Unlike a lot of songwriters, I don't fit the mold—you know the one where you constantly have to work at a job you hate to be able to put food on the table while you're waiting for a big break. If I want, I can walk away from the computer and spend all of my time writing music. Neither choice is conducive to meeting people and building romantic relationships. While many people are on date nights on the weekends, I usually meet up with a group of local songwriters, and we collaborate to help each other write what we hope to be the next hit song. That's probably not much fun for someone who doesn't want their big break in the industry. It's a dream that comes with more disappointments than rewards, but it's a dream that I can't seem to stop chasing."

"I get it. You've got to chase the dream, because the dream won't chase you," she added.

"That's the truth," Rich nodded in agreement. "I've had a thousand reasons to give up, but something keeps me going. You'd think rejection after rejection would wear most people down, but I keep telling myself I'm just one song away from making it big."

"And you might be. You did say that you've had a couple songs published, right? That must reinforce your dream, I imagine," Mindi said.

"Well, it is good for the ego," Rich smiled. "And, yes, a couple of my songs have made it as album fillers, and a few other placements, but that's as far as I have gotten. You can find them on YouTube, but they don't get any radio play, let alone top algorithm ranking."

"Here's to your fame and fortune," she said, lifting up her coffee cup as their server set their bill on the table. "And it looks like this is our signal that it's time to go."

"Let me," Rich said, reaching for the bill.

"No, I invited you. I'll pay," she insisted.

"You've been more than generous tonight, Mindi. Let me get the bill, I insist," he argued.

"Okay, thank you," she said graciously.

"No thanks necessary. All I ask is that you take a few minutes to listen to my song and give me your honest opinion. Do you still have my card?"

"I do," she answered, patting the front pocket of her purse. "I'll be happy to listen to it. And don't worry, I'll tell you what I really think."

"Good, don't worry about hurting my feelings. By now, my skin has gotten pretty thick," he smiled.

"I bet," she agreed. "Funny, isn't it, that I do everything I can to avoid the slightest criticism in my job, and you're the exact opposite, opening yourself up to it over and over again? Sometimes, I'd like to be a little more like you and worry less about what other people think."

"I know. The music business does have a lot of ups and downs, doesn't it? What I wouldn't give for a steadier rhythm now and then," he said as they walked out of the restaurant.

***

Late the next morning, Rich received Mindi's text message.

Rich, after listening to your song, I have to be honest and say that I'm not feeling it. It's not doing anything for me, which disappoints me because I did enjoy the one song I heard before. But this one is not for me. Thanks for the opportunity to give feedback.

Mindi

In disbelief, Rich read the text again. His initial disappointment quickly turned to defensiveness—could they possibly be talking about the same song—the same song that he truly believed was the best chance he'd ever had to have a hit song under his belt?

Needing an explanation, he texted her back.

"What didn't you like? The melody or the lyrics?"

Her response was short and immediate.

"Sorry, it just didn't resonate with me."

Taking a few minutes to let her curt reply sink in, he became offended, and in reaction, he jotted off a reply that didn't hold back his feelings.

"Thanks, but I think there are a lot of people who would disagree with your opinion. I should know. I am a songwriter, and you're not."

Before taking a second to think twice, he hit send and didn't regret it. Who was she to criticize him? Sure, she was a concert producer, but did she know anything about songwriting?

When Mindi read his reply, she sighed and tossed her phone on the table. Instantly, she wanted to kick herself, not because she'd stated her honest opinion, but because she'd allowed herself to become friendly with Rich, a songwriter who obviously was interested in how her career could benefit him. She knew better than to mix business with pleasure, something she'd never done in the past. It was a rule she'd imposed on herself. She'd crossed the line when she invited Rich backstage to meet the band, and she'd taken a giant step over it again when she invited him to join her for breakfast. When he'd asked her to listen to his song, she agreed, expecting that his experience in the music world had thickened his skin, but obviously it hadn't.

I went out of my way and made an exception for this guy, and this is the thanks I get. I guess no good deed goes unpunished. It's my day off; I don't have time for this, she thought to herself as she silenced her phone and walked away from it and their conversation, returning to the game she was playing with Rose.

3

RELATIONSHIPS

Relationships are the most significant factor impacting and influencing every aspect of our life.

W hile music played an integral part of both of their lives, that was the only similarity between Rich and Mindi. They each had different goals. More than anything, Rich wanted to write that mega hit song that he'd dreamed of since the first day he picked up a guitar. Sure, he'd had some success. Two of his songs had been published, and while they had fed his ego, his success was nowhere near the magnitude that he longed for.

Mindi, on the other hand, had already achieved her professional goals. She was an acclaimed concert producer who was well respected by artists and bands around the world. Yet, she struggled internally, wondering why her successes weren't mirrored in her personal life. It had been years, since her daughter was born, that she'd had a romantic relationship, and truth told, there were no prospects in sight. When did she have the time to even meet people? She worked long hours, and because she felt guilty about leaving Rose with her parents so often, every minute of her time away from work was spent with her.

Mindi knew something needed to change. Her father had indicated he was ready to retire and had given her subtle hints, reminding her that her parents had a lifelong goal of being able to travel in their golden years. Lately, this had been on her mind as she contemplated what their absence would mean to her and her daughter, Rose. There was no way she would feel comfortable leaving her with people she didn't know. There weren't too many people in the world that she trusted or even allowed to enter her intimate family circle. For that reason, she never mixed her personal life with her professional life and had spent her entire career making sure there was a firm line between the two. It was one reason why she had accomplished so much in her role, but it was also the reason for the potential turmoil she faced at home.

Rich also had enjoyed a successful career as a stockbroker in Los Angeles, managing sizable portfolios for his clients. While he wasn't passionate about his job, his position had enabled him to live comfortably and be able to afford to pursue his real passion: songwriting. Lately, though, that wasn't enough. He wanted more than a paycheck. Rich longed for something more fulfilling in his life and, in his opinion, every song he wrote had the potential to bring him one step closer to finding whatever that was.

He truly believed that fate had interceded to make that happen when he met Mindi Rhodes after the concert. It had been the first time he'd been bold enough to make his way backstage, and he couldn't believe his luck when she invited him to meet the band and then accompany her for a bite to eat. Everybody who was anybody in the business knew her name, and a connection with her could be the one ticket to breaking big into the industry. Of course, he wanted to take advantage of it.

Unfortunately, her response blindsided him. Where was the woman who had been so pleasant and, yes, friendly the night before? There wasn't a single sign of her in her text messages; that was for sure.

Torn between anger and disappointment, he sought validation by listening to his song over and over in an attempt to see if there was something he was missing, but that didn't change his opinion. In his eyes, he still had a hit on his hands, regardless of her opinion, which he reminded himself was just that ... an opinion.

Yet, her words gnawed at him, so much so that he knew he couldn't let it rest. And he knew just who to turn to—his father, the one person he could trust to tell him the truth.

An hour later, he was sitting across the table from his dad, as he'd done countless times before. He'd turned to his father all of his life for support, guidance, and his honest feedback. He had inherited his love for music from his dad, who had owned his own radio station. As a kid, he'd spent countless hours at the station, learning how to use the equipment and listening to the top hits that were aired. When he'd wanted to learn how to play the guitar, his dad encouraged him and signed him up for lessons. When he wanted to pursue songwriting on a full-time basis, it was his dad who advised him not to quit his day job just yet.

"You need a steady paycheck, son. Work and save your money until the day you can afford to take that risk," he'd said.

And Rich had listened, as he usually did to his father's advice. Through the years, he'd found that his dad was usually right, too.

"You seem a little riled up, son. What's going on?" the older man asked as he focused keenly on his son through his glasses.

"I guess I am, Dad. I just got a rather blunt rejection for one of my songs, from the concert producer I met last night, and I have to say that I don't agree with her. Will you do me a favor and listen to it and let me know what you think?" Rich asked.

Neither one made a sound during the 2 minute, 35 second track. When it was over, Rich turned to his dad and asked the ultimate question:

"Now, Dad, before you tell me what you think, I want you to read what this woman, Mindi Rhodes, sent me," he said, pulling out his phone and sharing the texts.

His father was silent as he read the texts, then he sat the phone on the table and slowly took his glasses off.

"Well? What do you think? Rather harsh, wasn't she?" Rich asked.

"Well, she didn't mince words. So, tell me, what's your problem with this? The rejection or the way it was worded?"

"I guess both. I mean, we had a good time the night before, even though we'd just met. She even invited me backstage, and we went out to breakfast at the end of the night," Rich answered.

"Ah, so having just met her, it's safe to say that you don't really know each other. You don't really have a relationship," his father said. "Perhaps, this is the real problem."

"What? I don't get it. What are you talking about, Dad?"

"Rich, you either have a relationship *to* someone or something or a relationship *with* them. There is a difference. Look at us, for example. You were related *to* me from the moment you were born, but from that time, you have a relationship *with* me. However, I don't believe you have a relationship *with* this woman, Mindi, at all. On the other hand, you do seem to have a relationship with your song. Perhaps what happened here was that you believed that your relationship with your song transferred to Mindi, but it did not."

"Go on, I'm listening," Rich prodded.

"What I'm saying is that an omelet and a cup of coffee do not constitute a relationship. After spending a brief amount of time together, I think you might have expected her to respond differently, perhaps more favorably because she knew you. However, her response was quite short and to the point. It's obvious that her response was all business, and she didn't take into account any relationship with you other than one that was from a purely professional standpoint," his father suggested.

"So, you're saying that I was the one in the wrong?" Rich's tone was once again defensive.

"I will say that I think the conversation might have gone differently if you had responded to her, rather than reacting to what she said," the older man offered.

"But I did respond…"

"Wait a minute, son. Remember, it's not always what you say, it's how you say it. Let me explain. It all goes back to relationships. When you relate *to* something, you react to it, which leaves nowhere to go. However, when you make a connection and have a relationship *with* someone, you respond to it and that offers more of an exchange. There is a difference. You let your emotions and ego get in the way and reacted to her rejection of your song. Simply put, you took it personally, and I can see that by your knee-jerk reply," his father pointed out.

"Well, I do disagree with her, Dad. How do you think I should have handled it?" asked Rich.

"I think your best interests would have been better served if you'd taken the time to consider your words before replying. In that way, you would have thoughtfully responded to her, instead of reacting to her feedback. Like I said, your reaction tells me that you don't have a relationship with this person. Rich, you have a relationship with the outcome, but not the person, and it shows. You expected more than you should have, but those expectations were based on false premises."

Rich sat silently and let his father's words sink in. As usual, he knew his dad was right. Based on their initial connection, he did have high expectations, and he did take her opinion personally. If he was honest with himself, he knew that his reply to her was unfair. After all, he had asked for her opinion, and she had given it, even though he still didn't agree with it.

"Okay, Dad, I get it now. I was wrong, and Mindi didn't deserve my reply. I think I owe her an apology for that. But you still haven't told me what you think of my song," Rich pointed out.

"Well, I'm not an expert, but I think I have to agree with Mindi. Although I wouldn't state it so bluntly, I don't think the song is there just yet," his dad said.

"Really?" Rich sighed, wishing his father's feedback had been more favorable. "Can you tell me where it could be improved upon?"

"Rich, just as with Mindi, I can't put my finger on any specific thing and tell you to work on it. But I can tell you that I don't think you've established a connection with your song," his dad said thoughtfully.

"What? I'm more connected to this song than any song I've ever written, Dad, and I've written hundreds!" Rich exclaimed.

"Once again, Rich, I'm talking about relationships. You are related *to* your song because you gave birth to it, but you don't have a relationship *with* it just yet. I think you're mistaking a connection with the outcome for a connection with the song," his dad suggested. "If you want me to tell you what's wrong with your song, I can't. That's because it's not about what's there … it's about what's not there," his dad said.

"Not there? What are you talking about, Dad?"

"Son, relationships are a factor impacting and influencing every aspect of our life, personal and professional, and they have a beat, a tempo, and a rhythm. From my point of view, you haven't been living in sync with that rhythm. I told you once not to quit your day job, but you're at a place now where you have the money and the ability to pursue what you really want. Perhaps it's time for you to go all in. Rich, I'm inviting you to get curious, get out of your head and stop focusing on fame, leave your ego at the door, and write from your heart. Feel the rhythm; that's where you'll find what's missing. That's where you'll discover what's missing in your song and, perhaps, in your life."

While his father's wise words were spoken firmly, Rich knew they were spoken with love and his best interests at heart.

"I hear you—there's something missing," Rich said, unable to hide his frustration.

"And only you can figure out what that is. Your song is your baby, and everything that is in it comes from inside of you. When you figure out what's missing in your life and in your heart, maybe then you will be able to express it in your songs."

His father's words gave him a lot to think about on the drive home, a trip he knew by heart. As he recalled their conversation, he became more uncomfortable with his father's words about connecting from his heart, and he came to the realization that, as usual, his dad's insights hit the mark. Maybe there was something missing—that one thing that would make all the difference in his songs.

He had always thought that the missing link was having the right connections, and he had to admit that he had hoped that Mindi would be the key that would unlock those doors. Sadly, he had to acknowledge the fact that he might have blown it.

Thinking of Mindi, he reminded himself to apologize for his reply. Stopping for a passing train, he spent several minutes thinking of the best way to word his response.

Just before the crossing gates rose, he got a glimpse of the caboose pulling up the rear of the freight train. The bright yellow graffiti sprayed on it depicted only one word: RESPECT.

RESPECT

*In the **Rhythm of Respect**,*
we show up and we're present, we listen, we build
trust, and lead with compassion and authenticity.

*When we bring **Respect**,*
our relationships are collaborative and empowered!

4

L I S T E N

Active listening is a full-body experience and increases the possibility of hearing the music beneath the words.

When he got home, the first thing he did was take out his phone to make amends with Mindi, but unlike writing lyrics, the words didn't come easily. For nearly an hour, he penned different variations of an apology, but in the end, they all fell short of what he wanted to say. Finally, he accepted the fact that there were no words that could undo the damage that had been done. Regardless, Rich knew it was his mess to clean up, so he quickly thumbed in what he hoped was an acceptable apology.

"Mindi, my reply to you was rude and uncalled for. I do appreciate your professional opinion and feedback. Please accept my apology."

Almost holding his breath, he waited for a reply that didn't come for an uncomfortable two hours. When the text came through, he picked it up immediately, anticipating her response more than he thought.

Her words were few and to the point. Her text simply read, "Thank you. Good luck."

Disappointed, he knew it was obvious that there was no invitation in her reply to continue their conversation. If anything, it was obvious that their communication was over.

Judging himself, he knew that he had sabotaged the connection and the possibility of a new friendship. It struck him that this wasn't the first time that he'd been in this situation. He also realized that it was a once-in-a-lifetime introduction, and he wouldn't be given another opportunity to meet a mover and shaker powerhouse like Mindi in the near future. Stockbrokers who worked online and amateur songwriters didn't have access to people like her and their broad network.

There's no turning back, he thought.

Then a lightbulb went off, and he had another thought.

I can move forward! If I want to get serious about music and actually fulfill my goal, it's up to me. I might have screwed this up with Mindi, but there are others out there who have connections and can help me. And I know the best place to find them!

Two weeks later, he closed his front door and checked to make sure it was locked one last time before tossing his suitcase into the back of his rental sedan. Choosing to rent a car for the trip, instead of flying, was a strategic move that he hoped would give him an opportunity to clear his head and leave some space for some much-welcomed inspiration along the way. Putting the car in reverse, he backed out of his driveway and didn't look back as he began the journey that would take him across the country to his ultimate destination, Nashville, Tennessee.

Thanks to interstate highways, the drive was an easy one, and before he knew it, he was on the last leg, taking the exit for I-24 off of I-57, which would take him straight into the Music City. It was a trip he'd taken before. The first time, he had been 12 years old when he accompanied his father on a business trip to meet with a few record labels that were promoting their artists. He had been so impressed, not only with the city, but also with the respect that his father had been shown by some renowned publishers and producers on Music Row. He could still remember beaming with pride over the fact that his dad was an important part of the industry, and that's when he vowed that one day, he, too, would follow in his father's footsteps and make his own success right there on Music Row.

Intentionally avoiding the heavy traffic in downtown Nashville, which he presumed was flooded with tourists, he headed southwest. His destination: 16th and 17th Avenues, or what was otherwise known as the Historic District, but what Rich fondly thought of as the songwriting capital of the world. It was home to record labels, radio stations, and recording studios. Some like RCA Studio B had been designated to be historic landmarks, and their contribution to the music industry was, therefore, preserved for decades to come.

After checking in at the hotel, he visited the sites and walked the streets that surrounded Music Row, some of which he remembered from previous visits, but others that were unfamiliar and appeared to be new monuments, museums, and eateries in the district. Before long, he found himself standing outside a building that housed the office of the music publisher that had marketed two of his songs—one to an up-and-coming artist who had included it on his first solo album and another that was featured in the background of a made-for-TV movie. Neither became a household hit, but they did validate for Rich that he had talent and gave him a glimpse of a promising career as a songwriter.

Knowing that it was unlikely that there would be any producers or record labels that would give him any time, he'd reached out to his publisher, Stu Stone, congratulating him on his latest article in the trades and letting him know he was going to be in town and would enjoy the opportunity to talk with him if he had time. Stu replied with an invitation for Rich to join him for lunch. "Meet me at my office at 11:30," he'd said.

At 11:25 on the dot, Rich pushed open the doors and gave his name to an inquiring receptionist.

"Stu will be with you in just a moment," she smiled.

As if on cue, Stu's jovial voice entered the room.

"Rich, my man, it's good to see you; it's been a few years," he said. "What brings you to Nashville?"

"Well, I've made up my mind to get serious about songwriting, so here I am. And of course, I couldn't come to Nashville without seeing you," Rich answered.

"I'm glad you did. So how about lunch? How does The Row sound?" Stu asked.

For more than three decades, The Row Kitchen and Pub had been an icon in Nashville. Not only was it known for its cuisine, it was also credited for its part in shaping Nashville's music industry. The live music played at The Row had introduced and launched the careers of artists and bands that had become superstars, and it was a place where songwriters were given equal credit with the written tribute, "We pay homage to the Working Class Poets of Nashville."

Did The Row sound good to Rich? Of course, it did. Any songwriter would be considered to be out of his mind to refuse that invitation.

After making small talk and placing their orders, Stu came right out and asked Rich a question.

"So, I don't think you came all this way to break bread with me, Rich. You got a song you want to pitch?" he asked.

"Well, now that you mention it, I do have a song. Well, I *did* have a song," Rich stammered.

"Do? Did? I'm confused," Stu said.

Rich spent the next few minutes telling the publisher about sharing his song with Mindi, making sure he left out the part where he snapped at her opinion.

"Anyway, it made me realize that if I want to be a successful songwriter, and I do, I need to do something more. What I'm doing isn't working, after all. I guess I thought if I came to town and talked to folks like you, I could figure it all out," he confessed.

"Ahhh, I see. I can see where you might have gotten your hopes up with Mindi—she certainly has connections," Stu nodded. "Well, if you want to know anything about music or songwriting, this is the place to be. I assure you there's no shortage of people here who will be happy to tell you that they know everything there is to know about music. This town might be the music capitol of the world, but it's also the rejection capitol. Unfortunately, very few of those rejections come with constructive criticism."

Rich knew just what Stu was talking about. He'd pitched a fair share of songs that had been rejected. While he respected the time they took to listen, some hadn't responded at all, and those that did usually didn't give a reason.

Just then, a man approached their table.

"Hey, Stu, I'm glad I ran into you. I want to talk to you about one of the songs you pitched last month. Can you drop by tomorrow, let's say about 10 a.m.?" the man asked.

"Absolutely, Teddy," Stu agreed. Then looking at Rich, he continued, "Rich, this is Teddy, he's the senior producer at Intention Studios. Ted, this is Rich, he's one of our songwriters and is visiting Nashville for a week or two."

After the two men shook hands, Teddy extended his invitation to Rich. "If you want to come along in the morning with Stu, I'll have someone give you a quick tour so you can see what's going on in our neck of the woods."

"That'd be great!" Rich enthusiastically agreed.

Once Teddy left, Rich sat in awe.

"I can't believe I just got to meet the great Teddy Alden! And I got invited to his studio!"

"It is definitely a privilege, and I'm sure you won't take it for granted, Rich. Teddy is a very busy man in a very demanding role, and if he offers you his time, appreciate it. If he offers you his advice, pay close attention and humbly accept it. The man knows his business. He knows what he's talking about, and he's one of the most respected professionals on Music Row. When he talks, people listen," Stu informed him.

"Oh, I get it. I promise I'll give him the respect he deserves," Rich replied.

The next morning, Teddy took a moment to talk with Rich.

"Stu said you're a songwriter. Have you had any success?" he asked.

"A little," Rich answered, giving him the names of the two songs that had been recorded, as well as the movie and a jingle that had been picked up for a TV commercial. "Right now, I'm planning on kicking it into a higher gear and turn my songwriting into a career."

"Looking for an invitation to play at the Bluebird Café?" he laughed. "So is every aspiring artist and songwriter in the nation. Some make it there, some don't. The best way to make it happen is to listen and learn."

"I'm listening. What's your advice for a guy like me?"

"Well, I haven't heard your songs, but I have mentored dozens of songwriters just like you, and I'm going to tell you the same thing I've told them. I've seen countless songwriters who are dying to get their songs in the right hands and hear their opinions, but when they don't like what they hear, they get defensive. But if they would just be present and listen to what is being said, they'd realize that the feedback was helpful, even valuable," Teddy shared.

Nodding, Rich admitted, "Yes, I've been guilty of that once, maybe twice."

"It's a natural reaction, but it doesn't serve anyone well. We know that songwriting is an art, but so is listening, especially when it comes to music," Teddy explained.

"But what if the feedback you get is negative, and the person fails to provide you with a reason or tell you what's wrong with it?" Rich asked.

Teddy shrugged. "Perhaps it was because they didn't know what was wrong with it, either. Maybe they just didn't relate to it, or they can't put their finger on it. That happens. But when it does, I can tell you that I think I know the real reason."

"What's that?"

"When they listened to the song, it didn't move their heart or their feet. Every great song will do one of those things, and there are only a handful that have actually done both," Teddy pointed out. "I encourage you to listen to the songs of award-winning songwriters, really listen to them, and you'll see that they either move your heart or your feet, Rich."

"Interesting," Rich replied. "Tell me, in your opinion, is there a certain genre or chord progression, melody, or hook that'll move your feet more than another?"

"What you're talking about is the mechanics of songwriting. The music industry isn't about mechanics, Rich. Sure, a great song needs a great melody and lyrics, but songs need more than mechanics. They tell stories with emotion or rhythms in a way that create a connection and makes people want to listen or dance, not just once or twice, but over and over and over again. They're like an experience people want to relive every time they hear the song. Do you get what I'm saying?" Teddy asked. "You can't write about what you don't know and expect it to move other people, especially if it hasn't ever moved you."

"And that's what sets apart great songwriters from the rest?" Rich asked.

"Yes. Sure, they're talented, but they learn to listen to their gut, trust their instincts, they listen to other songs, they listen to publishers and producers and people who work in the industry, and they listen to their heart. Music is all about listening, Rich, which is why it's tough to break into the industry. Rather than using independent songwriters, we'd rather have a pool of songwriters on staff to turn to, because they listen and are in sync with what *we* want. They listen to trends and know what relates to the audience. They listen to feedback, knowing it's one way to put an average song over the top. If they want to survive in this industry, they don't do it because they have to — they do it because they're all in and want to improve. Some of my best relationships are with songwriters who have listened to my criticism and followed my advice. I give that advice because I have a great deal of respect for them and their craft," Teddy explained.

"Thank you, Teddy. I appreciate your time and advice," Rich said.

"Hey, you can thank me by writing a hit song. And when you do, make sure I'm the first one Stu pitches it to," Teddy laughed.

***

For the next few days, Rich listened to his songs through Teddy's lens and asked himself if it really moved his heart or his feet. In the end, his answer to both of those questions was a resounding "no."

Sure, he could tap his toes along to the melody, but now he could feel that the melody was mechanical, based on a pattern of numbers, which was one reason writing songs was enjoyable for him. He knew numbers. He worked with them all day, every day. Songs were crafted with numbers, as well. Overall, a song has time limitations, only so many minutes and seconds, that is, if it wants air play. A song has a specific number of verses, each verse has the same number of lines, which consist of so many syllables, all connected to a melody that was based on a number of beats. He could numerically dissect a song within minutes, and it was the first thing he took into consideration when he started to write one.

That's when he realized just what Teddy had been telling him. Rich heard what Teddy said, and now in reflection, he understood what Teddy meant.

In order for a song to move the heart or the feet, it had to touch people in a unique way. It created a relationship with the listener. In order to do that, Rich needed to write about things that moved him. Then he could convey those experiences through his music.

But there was one problem. Rich didn't allow himself to "feel" very often—that's why numbers and mechanics were safe, and it had created success in his work as a stockbroker.

Listening to his own voice, Rich thought, *I know the numbers. Am I missing the very experiences I need in order to create the life and the songs I want, and more important, the songs other people want to listen to? I wonder what tomorrow will bring...*

RICH'S NOTEBOOK

Tomorrow is not up to someone else

The hope you have is hope that you can trust

The truth is that the future is up to each of us

***

In New York, Mindi was enjoying the success that Rich dearly wanted, but the demands, especially those she placed on herself, were beginning to take a toll on her. Her parents were observant and noticed it, as well, pointing out with increasing frequency that they felt she needed to take a break. At the minimum, they expressed their desire for her to cut back on her frequent travels. In the past month alone, she had spent three weekends away from Rose, and they'd noticed that their granddaughter was voicing her dissatisfaction about her mommy being gone so much. Each time, though, that they brought these points to Mindi's attention, she reacted, saying, "I'm doing the best I can to support my family." This frequent conversation only added to her stress!

In Mindi's mind, her job was vital to her daughter's future; therefore, she needed to make sure she did it well. She couldn't get why her parents didn't understand that everything she was doing was for Rose and their wellbeing. Instead, her parents worried it was having a negative effect on her.

While she wanted nothing more than to please her parents, who had been her right hand since Rose was born, she felt trapped, thinking that no matter what she did, it wasn't enough. To be successful, she knew she had to make sacrifices ... but she feared she was teetering on sacrificing her relationship with her daughter and her parents, and that scared her.

She knew something had to give ... but what?

5

TRUST

How you trust yourself is reflected in your relationships;
trust your instincts.

O nce she got out of the airport and the heavy traffic that surrounded it, Mindi sighed with relief. She always did when she returned from a trip, and this had been her third trip to the west coast in the last month. As she took I-87 north to her home in upstate New York, she looked forward to hugging and snuggling Rose and spending some time with her parents. She knew her frequent business trips were affecting her daughter, and that weighed on her every day.

Thank goodness she had her parents! It was hard enough to be a single parent, and the demands of her career didn't help. She knew she couldn't do this without them. She used to think that it would get easier over time—when Rose got a little older, it wouldn't be so hard to leave. The trouble was, though, that as Rose got older, it was actually becoming more difficult. Rose wanted more of Mindi's time, and while Mindi wanted the same with Rose, that was not possible at this point in her life.

Rubbing her temples, Mindi could feel another dreaded headache coming on. They, too, were becoming more frequent. She knew the cure, though, and that was a couple days off work and the opportunity to catch up on some much-needed sleep. Jet lag, hotel rooms, and late-night concerts weren't conducive to a good night's sleep.

As she rolled into her hometown, where she'd lived since the day she was born, Mindi felt some of the tension ease. The sense of familiarity and normalcy of home was a welcome relief. It was definitely worlds away from the concert life and the lifestyle of rock stars and their adoring superfans.

Rose ran to meet her as soon as she walked into the front door of her parents' house, where she and Rose had lived since her divorce. As she hugged her daughter, Mindi was surprised that her eyes welled with tears. Using the back of her hand to wipe them away, she managed to keep her daughter from noticing, but it didn't escape her mother's watchful eye. She'd never been able to hide anything from her. They had always had a sixth sense about each other.

"What's wrong, honey?" her mom asked, genuinely concerned.

"Nothing, just a bit overtired—and glad to be home. Seems the trips get longer each time, at least they feel that way," Mindi said, attempting a weak smile.

Picking Rose up and nose-to-nose with her, she asked, "How about a book before bedtime?"

The next morning, the smell of pancakes and freshly brewed coffee drew Mindi to the kitchen for breakfast with her parents and Rose, who was already dressed for school. While the food was fabulous, the "good morning, Mommy" from Rose was the most delicious part.

After Rose was safely on the school bus, Mindi and her parents talked over coffee.

"We're concerned that you work too hard. I wish you'd find a different job, something without so much pressure. It's not good for you to be crisscrossing the country all the time, and it's not good for Rose, either," her mom said.

It was the same discussion they'd had many times. However, this time, something was different—Mindi was starting to agree with her.

"I get what you're saying, Mom, but where else would I go? What else would I do? This is what I know, and I do my job well. And the pay is great."

Mindi's father chimed in, "At what expense? While we love Rose dearly, she misses you, and we all know that her grandparents are no substitute for her mom!"

"And when you are home, you're constantly getting calls to deal with the latest emergency. It's non-stop. Can't someone else handle some of those things when you're away from the office? How about Liz? Can't she do it?" her mom continued.

"Yes, Mom. Liz is excellent, and she does help me with a lot of things. It's just that there are some things that I prefer to do myself because I need to make sure…"

"I know, I know, You don't trust anyone else, and you need to make sure it's done perfectly," her mom interrupted. "You've always been that way, and it's starting to wear on you, Mindi, and on each of us. You can't be it all and do it all. Nobody can. Why don't you take some time off and empower your team to succeed using everything you've taught them? Now is probably a good time to tell you that your dad gave notice of his official retirement."

Mindi turned to her dad in surprise and hugged him. "Wow, Dad, that's a bold step!"

"We're thinking that we're going to start traveling this summer," her dad said.

Mindi's mom jumped back in. "That gives us time to plan for Rose's care, or, better yet, it gives you time to plan to come with us. You can take some time off, and we'll make it a family adventure. We all know that you need a vacation. It's only been … how many years? It would do you a world of good."

"Fat chance," Mindi chuckled. "There's no way I could just pack up and go. Everything would have to come to a standstill for that to happen."

"You could, and you can. Trust me on that," her mom remarked.

Mindi did trust her mother and, of course, her father. In fact, they were the only people she'd trusted with Rose since she was born, almost seven years prior. She didn't trust any other people, with her daughter or with her professional responsibilities. At work, she held herself fully accountable for everything, even the most minor details. Even though staff members who had been with her a while were more than capable, Mindi took it upon herself to check and double check that everything had been completed, often to the frustration of her team.

She also didn't trust anyone with her feelings. Mindi wasn't one to make close friends or to even have one confidant that she turned to. On a rare occasion, she connected with a mentor who opened the door to her career. As an only child, she was used to going at it alone. "You're strong," was her father's constant reminder, one which frequently ran through her head. And she had proven time and time again that she was just that. Professional relationships never crossed the line into her personal life, and while she was friendly with colleagues, she never socialized with the people she worked with outside of business-related events and functions--never. To do so would leave her vulnerable, and she wasn't about to subject herself to that.

After spending a quiet evening with Rose, her mother's words haunted her, and she wondered how she was going to find someone to take care of her daughter once her parents began their adventures. Yes, she wanted them to have the freedom to enjoy this season in their lives. At the same time, she shuddered with fear at the thought of not having them around daily, particularly since Rose loved them and they all had such a trusting, special connection!

While Mindi should have been exhausted, she was now unable to sleep. Wanting to find a way to shut off her mind, she looked for a book, a magazine, anything that would divert her attention. That's when she recalled a book that a fellow passenger was reading on the plane that day—*The Universal Relationship Rhythms*. Curious what it was about, she searched online and read the book summary, which fascinated her. On a whim, she quickly ordered the digital version and waited a few minutes for it to download.

She was a few chapters into the book when she returned to work at the beginning of the week. Already, she'd learned so much about relationships and had actually started to recognize some of her own patterns and tendencies and how they impacted the relationships she'd had with the people she led on her team.

She saw their potential and expected excellence from each team member to rise to her vision of them.

Polite and professional, Mindi often acknowledged the team along the way. Now she wondered if it was enough. At the same time, Mindi was closed, and her own insecurities showed up as being distrusting and controlling, versus trusting and empowering.

She did know that the team looked up to her, and they were confident that she would never subject them to failure. To do so would reflect poorly on them and her own outcomes as a leader, and that wasn't an option at all. She thought her team trusted her, and they knew that she'd respected them and had their backs—didn't they? Now, she wasn't sure.

The book also discussed romantic relationships, which she didn't have and didn't anticipate having anytime soon, as well as relationships with friends and acquaintances, again something that was lacking in her life. What she found most interesting was the fact that the book delved into the most important relationship, the relationship she had with herself, and on that note, she felt like a square peg attempting to fit into a round hole—she just couldn't identify with any of the relationship scenarios that she read about. She could only relate to the fact that she did not have them.

When she returned to the office that day after being gone for weeks, everyone came by to say hello. They seemed happy to see her, then they went about their work as usual. For Mindi, however, this day felt very different. She was suddenly present in a different way and felt that she had become a spectator in her own life. Like a third party, she was now curiously observing her behaviors with her team and coworkers and noticing how they responded to her. And she found she didn't like what she saw.

It was immediately evident to her that she was micro-managing everything, often reacting, versus responding. For the first time, it occurred to her that she wore her strength as a badge of honor, often without compassion. Was it because she didn't trust her team, who had been trained by her to do their jobs? She took nothing for granted, and for the first time, she wondered if her team resented her for that.

As she listened to her team's updates, she thought, *I have amazing people around me, they're good at what they do, so why don't I trust them? What indication or evidence is there for me not to trust them? Or as the book says, maybe it's not that I don't trust them—maybe I don't trust myself.*

There it was! She worried most about disappointing people and recognized that was at the core of her distrust. If she was strong and always stayed on the details to get it right, no one would be disappointed.

That night as she reflected on the relationships in her life, she also realized that she'd only had one real friend when she was growing up. Jamie was her complete opposite—while Mindi was reserved, Jamie was an open book. If she felt something, she showed it. If she had an opinion, she stated it. If she could trust anyone to tell her like it was, it would be Jamie.

The two hadn't seen each other since Jamie married her college sweetheart, after reconnecting a few years prior. She moved with him to Denver, where she taught junior high. They still kept in touch on social media and sent a text now and then. On a whim, Mindi picked up the phone and called her old friend.

"Mindi, is it really you?" Jamie's voice was both surprised and excited.

"Yes, it's me. How have you been?" Mindi asked.

"Oh, you know how it is. It's crazy and amazing all at once! I teach a classroom of 21 twelve-year-old kids and then come home to take care of my two little ones. We're always on the go. How about you? You still traveling all over the place, putting on concerts with rock stars? How's Rose and your folks?" Jamie laughed, as she paused momentarily to catch her breath.

"All good, and yes, I'm still producing concerts," Mindi chuckled.

"I want the whole scoop! Have you fallen in love with a recording artist? Maybe a lead singer?"

"No to both, Jamie. You know me, my job is strictly professional," Mindi answered.

"Not even a drummer, Mindi? Well, I'm not surprised—you've always played it safe," Jamie pointed out.

"I'm not looking for a romantic relationship ... or should I say one has not found me. I haven't met anyone I'm interested in, even if I was interested, which again I'm not."

"That's because you're so guarded, always have been. I'm amazed you let me in to your life when we were kids. And you've always had an excuse. You're too busy studying, too busy working, too busy being Rose's mom."

Mindi jumped in. "She's a great kid by the way, just missing her mom a bit lately. And I'm starting to feel the pressure."

"You need to get out and live a little! There's a whole world out there and a lot of people in it, including one for you, but you're still afraid to take a risk, allowing your past to rule you," Jamie said.

It was exactly as Mindi had pictured—Jamie was still as outspoken as Mindi remembered. It was why she'd called her, knowing that if anyone would be brutally honest, it would be Jamie. She trusted her.

"Are you still happy with your job, Mindi?" Jamie asked, this time, with a hint of concern.

"Yes, I still love my work. Even if I didn't, it's not like there are tons of openings for concert producers," she laughed. "It reminds me of a quote I just read in a book about relationships. It says, 'Trust that where you are now is where you're meant to be,' so I guess I'm in the right spot—for now," Jamie agreed.

"But where you're meant to be yesterday or today might not be where you're meant to be tomorrow," Jamie added. "Change can be good. Have a little faith and trust that it can actually be positive. Look at me—I left everything I knew and moved out here and created a whole new life, and I wouldn't trade it for anything in the world. I'd love for you to have that, too."

"Someday," Mindi replied softly. "For now, I can't just up and leave my career or my home."

"Why not?" her friend challenged her.

"Well, I won't leave a great paying job without having another one locked in first, and I'd need to find someone to help me take care of Rose when I travel, since my parents are planning to start their own travel adventures, now that Dad's retiring, and I'd need..."

"No, Mindi. You're wrong. You've spent your life and career showcasing and highlighting everyone else. There will never be a perfect time. *This* is your time. You have everything you need. You see, everything you need is inside you—the rest will come. Trust me on that. Now, I'm not sure, but the fact that you called tells me something more is going on. Am I right?"

"No, not really…" Mindi replied, denying her friend's question, although Jamie could sense a lack of confidence in her voice.

"Okay, so, you don't have to tell me what it is, but I will tell you the same thing I tell my students," Jamie said.

"What's that? I'm listening," asked Mindi.

"Always trust your instincts. If something is telling you that you need to make a change or that something's not right, listen, respect it, believe it. Mindi, I know for a fact that when you are present and listen to your instincts, they will never fail you! That's how you've become the success that you are, and that's what kept you and Rose safe when you left Shane. Your instincts didn't steer you wrong then, and they won't do it now. Follow your gut and make your choices from that place. Follow your heart and stop listening to the crap in your head that says, 'No, that won't work,' or 'I'll do it later when everything is in place.' Trust that when you lead with your heart, your head will follow, and everything will align! Your instincts—they're there for a reason," Jamie spoke with the wise confidence that Mindi admired, before she heard a child cry.

"Hey, girl, listen, that's Noah. I better go figure out what he needs," she said. "Feel free to call me anytime. I do miss you. Don't be such a stranger."

"Go take care of your little guy," Mindi said. "And Jamie..."

"Yeah?"

"Thank you. I mean that."

***

While Mindi was stepping out of her comfort zone to reach out to her old friend, Rich was pursuing opportunities during his travels to meet and write with new people in the hopes that they could provide the missing link that would transition him from a full-time successful stockbroker to a full-time successful songwriter. Ironically, as Mindi was being pressed to reduce her travels, Rich was on the hunt for new places to go and people to meet. He knew that his dream was somewhere out there—he just had to find it.

Because he had the privilege of working remotely, travel was an option that didn't interfere with his career. However, the one thing that held him back and continually drew him back home was his father—his best friend and close advisor. Theirs was the only relationship he'd had throughout his life that had lasted. He had an immense respect for his dad. As he contemplated the many lessons his father had instilled in him over the years, Rich had to wonder why his life was missing other friends who he could confide in.

6

CHOICES

How you choose to give is how you choose to live.

Later that week, Mindi took her book, *The Universal Relationship Rhythms*, to bed, hoping to read a chapter or two before she dozed off. She was finding the book to be intriguing, and it was making her take a hard look at her relationships—and her life—in a different light. In doing so, she found herself questioning her role in all of the relationships she'd had, as well as the relationships that were lacking. How was she showing up in them?

Initially, the title piqued her interest because of its reference to music, something which, of course, was predominant in her life. But she knew that within that world, her relationships didn't carry emotional attachments. Always the ultimate professional, she'd been profoundly successful in avoiding any perception of favoritism or improper relationships with any member of her team or the artists and musicians they served.

Being honest with herself, though, she was more interested in learning about the "universal relationship rhythms" in her personal life. Lately, instead of focusing on the abundance in her family life, she felt the lack of relationships had become more noticeable to her, and she wondered why. What was it deep inside her, a yearning for something that was lacking but that was very much needed? Or was she just second guessing herself and the choices she'd made throughout the years? Hopefully, the book would provide her with some insight into the answers.

After 15 minutes of reading, though, Mindi was distracted by a sudden ache in her neck. As she reached her hand back to rub her muscles, she tried to return her attention to the book but found that her eyes couldn't focus on the words as she experienced a couple flashes of bright light right before her vision dimmed.

Putting the book down, she closed her eyes tightly and shook her head, as if to shake away whatever was happening. When she opened her eyes, it took about 20 seconds until she regained focus.

Wow, I must be more tired than I thought. The best thing I can do right now is to get some sleep, she told herself.

The fact that everything was fine the next morning validated her thoughts. She was simply tired and needed more sleep. Quickly putting the incident out of her mind, she turned her attention to packing her suitcase, yet again to prepare for a four-day trip back to the west coast. As Rose sat on her bed, a norm on days when

Mindi packed, they sang songs and shared silly jokes. At one point, Rose looked up and said, "When do I get to pack and go with you, Mommy?" Mindi's heart sank as she kissed Rose and promised, "As soon as we can plan, my love, as soon as I can." Rose, seeming satisfied, went back to singing.

The only opportunity Mindi would have to be off her feet for the next few days was during her flight to Los Angeles. She had snuck in an extra day with Rose and knew she'd pay a price for it in the days ahead. It would be all hands-on deck when she landed. *Well worth it*, she thought. She spent the time in air going over the details of the upcoming concert with her assistant producer, Liz, just as they had done countless times before.

After loading their luggage into their rental car, Mindi turned to Liz, who had been with her for three years.

"Are we good to go?" she asked.

Tossing the car keys to Mindi, Liz replied, "Yes, I made sure we have everything," she reassured her.

It was rare that they did not take a car service, but Liz had rented a car for this trip to get to some off-site meetings. Mindi said yes to the rental on one condition, "I drive from the airport." Mindi was not a fan of being a passenger and not being in control.

Neither spoke for ten minutes, and it was Liz who broke the silence.

"Mindi, can I ask you a question?"

"Sure. What do you need?"

"I don't need anything. I was just wondering how you manage Rose when you travel for work. Abram is almost nine years old, and he should be used to me travelling by now. But he still gets pouty when I leave. His dad is great with him, but what I hear most often is that he misses me. Sometimes I wonder if they both just want me to feel guilty. If so, I have to admit it works. I just wondered if Rose is like that with you, and how you may handle it," Liz shared.

Rose ... Rose was always off the table. Rose was hers, and she didn't share her with anyone but her parents. Talking about Rose was too personal. Keeping her eyes on the road to avoid looking at Liz, she tried to figure out how to respond without making her feel uncomfortable. After all, her question was innocent, and she was asking for advice. Before she responded, though, Mindi's thoughts went to the book she had been reading and her reflections. It was Mindi who wasn't willing to create a personal connection and share. Rose was a part of her world that others were never allowed to see, up until now.

While she was formulating a supportive response, suddenly, Mindi felt a sharp pain in the back of her head, and flashes of light danced before her. She blinked hard, hoping to make them disappear, but if anything, they became more frequent. Just as she had the night before, she shook her head from side to side, hoping to correct whatever was happening.

"Mindi? Mindi? Are you alright?" Liz asked.

"Uh, I'm having trouble focusing on the road," Mindi answered. "I think I have to pull over. You're going to have to drive."

Hitting the brakes, Mindi began to slow down and steer their car to the shoulder of the road, when suddenly, the bright lights vanished … everything went dark, and panic set in.

"Liz, I can't see! I can't see anything!"

But Liz didn't have time to respond before they were hit from behind and their car veered off the road, past the shoulder and into a ditch.

***

"Mindi, Mindi! Can you hear me? Wake up, now!"

"What?" she asked as her eyes slowly opened.

"Mindi, do you know where you are? You're in the hospital," a man answered.

"Can you see me, Mindi?" he asked.

"Um, yes, but you're blurry and everything is kind of dark," she informed the doctor before closing her eyes again. "It hurts to look."

"Where does it hurt?"

"My head. I have a terrible headache," she said.

"What happened?" she asked, confused.

"You were in an automobile accident. Your assistant said you were rear ended by a car on the freeway. Do you remember that?"

"Not really," Mindi moaned.

"Mindi, I want you to think. She told us that the last thing you said was that you couldn't see. What happened?" he asked.

"I'm not sure," Mindi answered as she started gaining some recollection of the events leading up to the accident. "Um, there were bright lights and a sudden pain in the back of my head. Then everything went dark, like somebody turned the lights off, and I couldn't see the road anymore."

"Okay, we need to make sure you don't have internal injuries from the accident, but so far it looks like you got lucky, though we're going to need to take some X-rays and a CT Scan. You might have a broken collar bone, judging by the bruising. Let me take a look at your eyes," he said, pulling a light out of his pocket.

Mindi winced at the irritation of the bright light shining in her eyes.

After a bustle of activity where Mindi was rushed to radiology for a CT scan of her head and X-rays to rule out a fracture, she found herself in a private room on the third floor of the hospital. Within a few minutes, Liz walked into the room.

"Mindi, how are you? I've been so worried!" she exclaimed.

"I've had better days. How are you? Did you get hurt?" Mindi asked as she looked at her assistant, who resembled a dark shadow, a figure without features, through her eyes.

"A little sore, but I'm okay. Don't worry, they checked me out from head to toe, just to make sure," Liz smiled.

"I'm so sorry, Liz. I didn't mean to cause an accident. I don't know what happened—it all happened so fast."

"You don't have anything to be sorry about, Mindi. You did everything right—you slowed down and had your turn signal on. You were pulling off to the shoulder when we were hit by the car behind us. I'm just glad you're okay," Liz said. "Oh, and I took the liberty of calling your mom. I thought you'd want her to know. She wants me to call her back as soon as we know what's going on."

"Thank you. Knowing my mom, she'll jump on the next plane. If she says anything, tell her I'm okay. I just need her to take care of Rose."

"I will … but, Mindi, she sounded really concerned. I wouldn't be surprised if she's already at the airport. But I will do my best to calm her. And don't worry about the concert. I'm on it—remember, I've been trained by the best, meaning you. And the venue has been great. They've offered any resources or support we may need. They were more worried about you than anything else. You have lots of fans in the industry! And I don't want you to worry about a thing—I promise you can trust us. We won't let you down," Liz reassured her, before saying that she'd be checking in on her often.

She'd almost forgotten about the concert and wondered if Liz was ready to step in and fly solo with such a big production. Dozens of reasons why she needed to be there crossed her mind, and with every one of them, her head throbbed just a little more. As her heart raced with anxiety and the throbbing in her head continued, she realized that Liz was her only solution at this moment. She had no choice—trust was the only answer.

As Liz turned to head out the hospital room, Mindi stopped her, "Thank you, Liz. I trust you. You've got this."

***

"Mindi, it looks like your collar bone *is* broken," the doctor said as he entered the room.

"My head is pounding, and everything is getting dark again," she moaned.

After the physician examined her again and asked more questions, he told her his preliminary diagnosis.

"They're called ocular migraines," he explained. "They're temporary and usually resolve on their own within an hour or so, but sometimes, if they're left untreated, they can last longer. In severe cases, if untreated, they could cause permanent damage to a person's vision. We need to observe you for a few days while we find the appropriate medication to manage your symptoms."

"I can't stay here for a couple days," she complained.

"You don't have a choice. Right now, you can't see, and I want to rule out the possibility that it could be something even more serious. It will take a few days to get all the test results back. Be patient with yourself!"

Little did the doctor know who he was talking to! A few days of bed rest would drive her stir crazy.

She was advised to give her eyes an opportunity to rest, which would reduce the constriction that causes the migraines. One of the nurses offered to bring her an eye mask and some headphones if she wanted to listen to music, but she found that music only made her worry about being at work.

"Do you like to read?" the nurse asked, trying to suggest an alternative to help her pass the time. "One of the ways I like to decompress after a 12-hour shift is to take a nice long bath while listening to an audiobook. I like listening to books so much now that I rarely read books anymore!" she said.

"Well, I was reading a book …"

A few minutes later, the nurse had downloaded the audiobook version of *The Universal Relationship Rhythms* onto her phone, and Mindi closed her eyes and listened.

As she listened to the narrator, she found that she was surprisingly getting more out of the book. Even though she couldn't see the words, she could hear the message more clearly.

There is a rhythm to everything in life, and if one thing is out of sync, it affects everything else. Your body is a perfect example. When something is neglected or injured, it affects your body. When your relationships are unhealthy, your mind will send you signals, and until you acknowledge and face whatever is not working, you cannot experience the state of contentment, harmony, and peace—the state where everything is in sync.

Be present to your thoughts; respect your body and what it is telling you. Your positive or negative thoughts are the gateway to your actions. And your brain can only process one at a time. When you tell yourself negative things, your actions will reflect that negativity. Listen to your heart and your mind. Trust what they are telling you. Trust is a choice, for it is in that choice that you create your own unique rhythm—the rhythm that empowers you to make all of your relationships, personally and professionally, the best they can be.

When you choose to act according to the rhythm of your relationships, you are choosing to make a positive and healthy impact on yourself and everything around you. Choice is ongoing. All relationships are about creating a connection to something or someone—your health, your business, your finances, your family, and your loved ones. Choose with awareness, while staying in tune with who you are.

The audio was interrupted when her phone rang, and she immediately recognized her mom's special tone.

"Hi, Mom," she answered.

"Mindi! I'm so happy to hear your voice! We've been so worried. How are you? What are the doctors saying?" her mom spewed out the questions without taking a breath.

"Calm down, Mom, and take a breath. I'll be fine. How is Rose?"

"She's fine, honey. She's really such a good girl. You, on the other hand, are another story! You're taking on too much, and now it's affecting your health. Mindi, I think this is a sign that you need to make some changes and get some rest," her mom pleaded.

"You know, we've already discussed this, and I told you why I can't do that right now. I have to support Rose, so leaving my job is out of the question. And besides, the doctor says that what I have is treatable with the right medication. It's just going to take a couple days, and I'll be home and back on the road before you know it," Mindi said.

"You stay there and listen to the doctors," her mom demanded. "You aren't going anywhere by yourself. I'm coming to you. My flight leaves first thing tomorrow morning and should arrive by lunch time."

"Mom, you don't need to do that. I'll be okay. I promise. I don't want to disrupt Rose's routine."

"Mindi, right now, you need someone to take care of you, and I know you won't admit it. So, like it or not, I'm coming. Get used to it! It looks like you don't have a choice."

Accepting that this was one argument she was not going to win, Mindi knew it would be futile to object. Instead, she focused on something her mother had said.

"That's strange. I was just thinking about choices as I was listening to an audiobook," Mindi shared.

"What is the title of the book?" her mom asked as she'd done dozens of times before—she and Mindi had long shared a common love for a good book.

"It's called The Universal Relationship Rhythms. I bought it because the title was catchy, but it's turning out to be very interesting," Mindi advised.

"I have that book on the shelf in the den. I bought it three or four months ago when it first came out, and I've read it twice since then. I was actually going to recommend that you read it, but I wasn't sure if you would make the time," her mom pointed out. "How far are you into the book?"

"I just finished listening to the part about choices when you called," Mindi answered. "And now you tell me that I don't have a choice."

"You always have choices, Mindi. But you cannot make the right choices if you don't allow yourself to consider any other options. How can you make a choice if you don't even see it in front of you?" her mom questioned.

"Well, right now I'm having a little trouble seeing much of anything," replied Mindi. "I have to admit that it would be nice to see Rose. Our time at home was so great, and I miss her already. Promise me that you won't say anything to her about the accident!"

"She's fine, and, of course, your father and I won't tell her. Besides, I'll only be gone for a few days. Before she knows it, we'll be back, and we both know how much she'll love her dedicated Grandpa time. So, I'll see you tomorrow, dear," her mom said so softly that Mindi could hear the worry in her usually strong tone.

After hanging up the phone, Mindi thought about what her mom had said and suddenly started to see a connection she hadn't seen before. *Hmmm,* she thought, *is it possible that I'm having these ocular migraines and losing my sight because other parts of my life are not in sync and out of rhythm? How ironic for someone whose career is devoted to delivering music to hundreds of thousands of admiring listeners! Here*

I've spent years listening to thousands of hit songs, and I know every word by heart ... I know how the artist uses music to touch hearts, but I don't have a clue what my heart and body are trying to tell me.

But if I want to make sure I can see again, it looks like I need to start respecting my body and listen to what it's telling me. Like Jamie said, I need to trust my instincts and base my choices on them.

Mindi had one problem with that—her heart had led her astray in the past, and she did not trust her instincts when it came to her personal life. When that happened, she had made a choice not to rely on them ever again. But her instincts were telling her that there was something else going on.

She wondered, *Why is this happening? Why now? What am I not seeing in my life ... and how can I figure out what it is?*

***

Still on the road, Rich was dealing with his own dilemma: to keep doing what he'd always done and hope he'd get a lucky break, or accept the fact that perhaps he'd been kidding himself, and he just didn't have what it took to be a hit songwriter. Neither choice held much promise. The former could take a lifetime to achieve, and the latter, well, he wasn't ready to entertain that one, just yet.

Unfortunately, though, Rich couldn't see another alternative or outcome. He didn't yet trust what was possible, and he didn't yet realize that the key to success was in recognizing that his choices were limited only by his mind and fears.

It was late when Rich sat down to write...

RICH'S NOTEBOOK

Each of us can stand for something good
Every time we rise, we elevate the place we live
We expand our souls by what we give...
Each of us...

RESPONSIBILITY

*In the **Rhythm of Responsibility**,*
we are intentional, we are committed, we communicate
clearly, and we stand accountable for our actions.

*When we are **Responsible**,*
expectations are aligned,
and our relationships are full of possibilities.

7

INTENTION

Intention is the fuel for ascension.

After spending more than a month travelling, writing, and collaborating with writers in Nashville, Memphis, and a few other cities, Rich was glad to be back in Los Angeles, which had always been home to him. Not only was he more familiar with palm trees than grandiose oak trees, but LA was about family. It was where his father was, and his father was the one person he respected, trusted, and felt connected to more than anyone else.

Stepping into the crowded airport terminal after exiting the plane, he decided to grab a quick cup of coffee, hoping it would help him avoid the crowd as the rest of the passengers headed to claim their luggage. After the barista handed him his drink, and just as he was sitting down, an announcement over the intercom caught his attention.

"Mindi Rhodes, please report to Gate 42. I repeat, Mindi Rhodes please report to Gate 42."

His head snapped from one side to the next. Mindi Rhodes? Could it be the same Mindi Rhodes that he'd met?

Instinctively, grabbing his drink, he rose from his chair and started walking in the direction of Gate 42, which, as luck would have it, was on the opposite end of the airport.

Knowing that he had quite a bit of distance to cover, Rich picked up his pace, scurrying around other passengers who were milling about or talking on their phone until it was time for them to board. Chances were slim that he would make it to Gate 42 in time to ascertain if the page was for the Mindi that he knew, but for some reason unknown to him, he was compelled to give it a try.

Slightly out of breath, he approached the gate and was immediately disappointed that he didn't see her.

"Can I help you, sir?" the gate agent asked.

"Uh, a Mindi Rhodes was paged to this gate a few minutes ago. I was hoping to catch her," he informed her.

"I'm sorry, sir. The plane is already loaded and ready for departure," she replied.

"Oh, okay. Thanks," he said, knowing there was nothing he could do. In a way, he was relieved. After all, Los Angeles International Airport was a hub of activity, and there were probably a dozen people named Mindi Rhodes. Shaking his head, he realized that it probably wasn't her, especially since she lived in New York.

And even if they had paged the Mindi he knew, what would he have said to her? That he rushed halfway across the airport just to say hi? Knowing how awkward that would be, he thought it was probably a blessing that he got there a moment too late.

Taking a sip of the coffee still in his hand, he started the long trek back across the airport. By now, he surmised, most of the passengers had likely retrieved their luggage. By the time he got to baggage claim, the crowd would be gone and on their way.

Luggage in hand, he made his way to the parking garage. Just as Rich opened his car door, an airplane made its way down the runway.

What he didn't know was that as he was going home, so, too, was Mindi.

Stepping outside the baggage claim door, hoping to quickly catch a cab, he noticed a sign posted on the concrete wall across the street, and the words caught his attention. It merely read: The Responsibility is All Yours.

Funny, he thought, I've been here dozens of times and have never seen that sign before. *The responsibility for what?* he wondered.

***

The next day, visiting his father was the first thing on his agenda.

"Hey, Dad. It's good to see you," he said, giving his dad a warm embrace.

"Hi, son. How was the rest of your trip and your flight?"

"It was an inspiring trip and an uneventful flight, which is good, I guess. How are things here at the old homestead? Any word from Tim or Terri?" he answered, inquiring about his two younger siblings. Twins, they were built-in best friends, and Rich had always felt he was outside of their circle, mostly because, as the oldest child, he'd been charged with the responsibility of looking after them, especially after their mother left.

"Nothing has changed around here, which is also good, I guess," his dad remarked with a grin. "And you know how it is. Terri calls every Sunday, when she has time. The kids have her and Grant running in circles with school and sports and dance. I talk to Tim when we can, usually when I call him. Based on the postcard that came last week, he and Jose' are doing well. You know them— they're still spending their time traveling to art shows, galleries, and festivals with their work around the southwest. Like you, they're still chasing their dreams."

Ignoring his father's reference to his dreams, Rich replied, "Next time, tell the little tykes that their favorite Uncle Rich sends his love."

His father noticed but didn't make any mention of the fact that Rich hadn't included his siblings in that message. The truth was, when the twins had moved to Arizona, it only validated Rich's belief that his relationship with his brother and sister was strained and disconnected … and the miles that separated them after their move exaggerated the lack of closeness to his siblings that he'd felt for a long time. While they'd initially kept in touch, their communication became more and more sporadic, and eventually, Rich stopped reaching out, feeling like he was trying to force a relationship with them.

Looking around, Rich was grateful to change the subject.

"Hey, Dad, it looks like you got yourself a new recliner," Rich mentioned, suddenly noticing a new chair in the corner of the living room.

"Yes, I did. I guess when you've been away, you notice things like that."

"Well, the old one was looking a little worn. Glad you decided to splurge and treat yourself."

"Well, I'm getting a little too old to travel across the country, like you, so I decided I could make things a little nicer around home," his father said.

"I'm glad you did. I forget sometimes how lucky I am that I can get away from time to time. I have the opportunity to work remotely from anywhere, and since I live alone, I don't have any other responsibilities. It does give me lots of come and go flexibility and the opportunity to pursue my songwriting career," Rich mentioned.

"Is that how you see it?" his father asked, raising a brow.

"Well, sure. Is there any other way?"

"Perhaps there is, son. Just because you don't have a family of your own or even a pet to take care of, that doesn't mean that you don't need to be responsible," his dad said.

"What are you saying, Dad?" asked Rich. "I am responsible. I work and pay my bills. I don't ask for help from anyone."

"I know you do, and the Homeowner's Association takes care of your lawn and landscaping. That's not what I'm talking about, though. I'm talking about being responsible in other areas."

"Such as?" Rich questioned his father.

"For instance, your songwriting. Let me ask, did you collaborate with other songwriters while you were in Nashville?"

"I did," Rich answered, waiting to see where his father was going with this.

"Okay, then. You are responsible for what you bring to those relationships, Rich. Every relationship you have comes with responsibility, whether it is in how you respond, engage, or support those people. I learned that in the radio business. I guess what I'm trying to say is that you are responsible not only for those relationships and your role in them, but ultimately, you are also responsible for the outcomes of those relationships. Remember how it went with … uh, that woman, the concert producer … what's her name?" his dad asked, snapping his fingers as he tried to recall.

"Mindi?" Rich answered.

"That's it! Now, I hate to say it, but you are responsible for the outcome of that relationship, too. As I recall, it wasn't such a good one, was it?" his father asked.

"No, it wasn't. But I did apologize. You know it's funny that you mention Mindi. When I was at the airport, they paged a Mindi Rhodes, and I wondered if it was the same one," Rich said.

"Was it?"

"I don't know. I looked, but I didn't see her," he answered.

"Did you want to see her?" his father inquired.

"I don't know. At the time, I guess I did, but I'm not sure why," Rich confessed.

"When you reopen that door, if you reopen it, remember that you are responsible for the response you will receive," his dad said.

"How so? How can I be responsible for *her* response?"

"Ultimately, the outcome of everything we do is the responsibility of a party of one—ourselves. Sure, you asked Mindi for her opinion. You aren't responsible for her opinion, but the relationship suffered because of what you are responsible for, and that is you—you and your reaction and response to it. Rich, the biggest responsibility we have isn't to our kids, spouses, jobs, or houses. No, it is being responsible for ourselves, first. When that happens, your relationships will improve, and you'll begin to see more and more possibilities," his father said.

"I say this," his dad continued, "because I think you're traveling to different places in an attempt to get a different outcome, when the truth is that geography won't make a difference. Let me ask you, when you were communicating with Mindi, do you think your reply to her criticism could have been construed as being overpowering? There's a difference between being empowered and overpowered. I've always said that empowered action brings dreams to life."

Rich sat and silently nodded as he was starting to understand what his father was saying.

"I think it's best to know your intentions at all times. And to be clear about why. Not only that, but it's also important that your intentions are clear at all times to the people around you. You cannot assume that they understand what you're expecting or striving for if you don't communicate your intentions to them. And let's not forget that you are accountable for what you bring to any relationship. If you can do that, no matter where you go or who you meet, you'll find that the outcomes sway in your favor more often than not."

Always a wise man, Rich listened, taking in his father's words. His father was often philosophical, and he'd always had keen insight. He didn't mince words; he merely spoke the truth as he saw it, always with the intent to do good, not harm. Knowing that, Rich was clear that his father believed he was telling him something he really needed to hear, for his own good. Rich wasn't sure he liked that because it left him pondering just what he had done in the past that he could have done differently. Was it his responsibility that he seemed to always fall short of his dreams? Believing that his dreams were just out of arm's reach made it easier to believe that his songs hadn't reached the right people yet. Rich's time on the road opened up a door to be more present and in tune with his life and open to possibilities.

"I think I get it, Dad. I'm just not sure where to begin," Rich replied.

"It's really not complicated, son. It's an inside-out job! How you're feeling inside is how you're showing up outside with others. It starts with a good relationship with yourself, which is what you need before you can expect good relationships or outcomes with the people you know. Only then can you have a relationship with your music, your career, your network, and your community. Know your intentions and what you want to accomplish. Be clear about why you want it, and don't let your ego rule you. Then you need to be accountable for everything you do or don't do. When you have a trusting relationship with yourself, you bring your best to the rest of the world. It took me a long time to learn that, and when I did, I saw changes in every area of my life, personally and professionally. That's what I want for you, too."

After a thoughtful pause, Rich spoke up.

"Is it possible that I was chasing my dream when I ran across the airport to see if it was the Mindi I know at Gate 42? That maybe I was still hoping that if she saw me, it would change something?"

"It could be. But I don't think you're ready. What was your intention if it was her? To have a chance to quickly say hi? Maybe give her another song to listen to? Why did you chase after the possibility of seeing her, and what outcome were you hoping for, Rich?"

"I don't know," he admitted.

"Then you're probably right and you were chasing your dream, but you weren't being responsible for your intention, actions, or outcomes. Your Nashville publisher, collaborating songwriters, or even Mindi aren't responsible for your dream, and neither is anyone else. The only one responsible for that is you. When you empower yourself, son, your actions will be empowered, and those dreams will come to life on their own. There won't be any need to run after them and hope they didn't fly away."

"I'll keep that in mind, Dad. And there's something else I want to be responsible for," Rich said.

"What's that?"

"Lunch. I've been wanting to go to The Hut and satisfy my craving for some jerk chicken and plantains. Want to join me? I'll buy," he offered.

"Sounds good, but I'll go easy on the heat. Otherwise, I'll be feeling it tonight, and I'll have to sleep in that recliner," he chuckled.

"Great! That was easier than I thought. I figured I'd have to talk you into it," Rich replied.

"Of course, it was easy. You stated your intention and the outcome you wanted. You empowered me to choose and take action, and you communicated it to me honestly. And, voila, you got the results you wanted. So, stop trying to make everything so hard!" his dad smiled.

***

Back in New York, after being released from the hospital in California, Mindi had every intention of turning her health around and restoring her vision. And that came with a price. For one thing, she had to succumb to the fact that she couldn't do it all on her own—she had limitations now. For the first time, she chose to let other people take over some of her responsibilities, and that left her feeling very uneasy and exposed, especially at work. She'd trained her team well, but the only person she had trusted up to this point to make sure every detail was addressed was herself. Having pulled off the concert that Mindi missed, Liz was now becoming a trusted member of Mindi's team.

On top of that, she had to accept even more support from her parents, who now had to do so much for her, especially since she couldn't drive. Her mom used this opportunity as proof that she needed to slow down. She'd overdone it and risked her health—and that wasn't fair to her, Rose, or them. Her parents had every intention of persuading her to see things their way … and she had every intention of proving to them (and herself) that she could still do it all.

The only thing she couldn't do was sit idly and lose control of everything she had worked so hard for. While the book she had been reading was making her more aware and reflective, she was still telling herself that if there was one thing she'd learned years before, it was that she never wanted to feel helpless ever again.

8

COMMUNICATE

When communication and expectations are aligned,
magic happens.

The Hut was a popular eating establishment, due to its authentic Caribbean cuisine and island décor … and because the patrons were always greeted by Winston, the chef/owner, who stood tall with colorful beads in his braided hair and a broad, infectious smile.

"Rich, man!" Winston exclaimed. "It's been too long. We missed you last month. I thought I'd see you when the Pepper Tribe was playing."

You know I love them, but I was out of town. Next time, though, I'll be sure to be here," Rich said to Winston, whom he had established a relationship with years before, both as a patron of his restaurant and as a fellow musician who admired Winston's musical abilities on those occasions when he joined live bands that entertained at The Hut on the weekends. "In the meantime, I'm ready for some of your famous jerk chicken."

A quick snap of Winston's finger summoned a server, who escorted them to a table for two.

"Enjoy," their server said as he sat a plate of jerk chicken in front of Rich and a plate of shrimp in front of his father. "Mild, just like you ordered."

"This looks sooo good. My mouth is watering already," Rich said as he dug his fork into the seasoned meat and took a bite.

Rich enjoyed the reggae music that was playing in the establishment while he enjoyed the rich, spicy flavors that were the hallmark of jerk cuisine. As he got lost in the food, his toes tapped in sync with the beat of the music.

A few minutes later, he pulled himself out of his enjoyment of the food and the environment and looked across the table.

"How's yours, Dad?" he asked. "Everything good?"

When his dad didn't answer right away, he leaned forward to see if something was wrong. That's when he noticed that his father's face was bright red and tiny beads of sweat were glistening above his brow.

"Is the food too spicy, Dad? Here," he said, pushing a glass of ice water toward him, "have a drink. It'll help."

After a quick sip, his father sat the glass down on the table and grimaced.

"You don't like the shrimp?" Rich asked, concerned.

"No, it's … it's not that. My chest," his dad said, suddenly struggling to speak as his hand clutched his chest. "It hurts to breathe."

Instantly concerned, Rich sprang to his father's side.

"Dad, are you okay?" he asked frantically. Then, without waiting for a response, he yelled, "Someone call 911! Hurry!"

Everything happened so quickly after that. The paramedics came and started an IV. They put an oxygen mask on his father and took his vitals. Rich knew it was serious by the way they rushed him out of the restaurant and wasted no time loading him into the ambulance. The mere thought of something being wrong with his father made Rich's heart race with fear.

In the emergency department, Rich listened intently when the doctor confirmed that his father was having a heart attack, saying time was of the essence. He needed to get to the heart Cath lab immediately so they could open any blockages or determine if he would need to have surgery.

"He's sedated right now," the doctor explained. "As his next of kin, I need your approval to perform the procedure."

Quickly glancing at the form in his hands, Rich could barely comprehend what was happening as he scribbled his signature at the bottom.

"We'll be taking him back in a minute," the doctor said. "We'll keep you updated throughout the procedure."

"Okay, what can I do?" Rich asked, feeling helpless.

"If he has other family members, you should probably notify them. I'm sure they'd want to know. Someone will come out and give you updates throughout the procedure," the doctor informed him.

Taking a seat in one of the chairs in the waiting room, Rich paused and took a couple deep breaths, a trick he'd learned as a performer to calm his nerves. Dreading reaching out to the siblings he rarely spoke to, his mind drifted as he contemplated what to say, with the anxiety of different outcomes popping into his mind. It was possible that this was a scare, nothing more, and there wasn't a need to alert his brother and sister ... just yet. But what if everything took a bad turn and their dad wouldn't make it through the procedure? Rich shook his head as if to erase that negative thought from his mind. Like it or not, Rich knew he owed it to them to let them know. It was their right to know, but still he procrastinated, buying time before placing the calls.

He had just about convinced himself to wait until he'd received an update before calling—at least that way he'd have something concrete to tell them—when the doctor appeared in the waiting room. After directing him into a small conference room, he told him that stents had been successfully placed to reopen two of his father's main arteries, as well as two other areas. They had saved his life, but damage had been done to his dad's heart that would require close observation, rehabilitation, and significant lifestyle changes.

"He's going to be limited in what he can do. And for the next couple months or so, he'll need assistance, at least until he can regain his strength. I know it isn't what you wanted to hear, but it could have been worse, and he's a strong man otherwise. It'll be a while before he's out of the woods completely, though," the doctor advised.

"Don't worry about that. I'll take care of him," Rich replied without hesitation. "As his oldest son, it's my honor and my responsibility."

To Rich, it was his responsibility alone. The twins were in Arizona and had lives of their own. In his mind, taking care of their dad was up to him, just as Rich had been charged with the responsibility of taking care of his brother and sister when they were growing up. While Rich had resented the twins' relationship with each other, he had never resented being the big brother and the one their dad always turned to. In fact, he prided himself on it.

That was something that hadn't changed, and Rich vowed that it never would. Not much had changed between Rich and his father throughout the years, but so much had changed in the last 24 hours. That morning, he'd looked forward to visiting his dad, and this afternoon, he was faced with the aftereffects of almost losing the only person he'd been able to turn to and truly trust.

He hadn't felt so alone since the day his mother had left, the day that had impacted all of their lives and their relationships with each other forever. Although he was just fourteen at the time, Rich stepped up and began to care for his brother and sister, who were four years younger.

Now, he owed it to his dad to let his brother and sister know about his condition. Rich realized it wasn't about what he wanted; it was about what his dad would want. In his mind, he recalled what his father had always said, "Family comes first, and when I go, you kids get to stick together."

Yet, this would be the first time that Rich reached out and communicated with either one of them in quite a while.

It wasn't a call he wanted to make at all. But as the oldest son, he stood in his responsibility.

Terri and Tim were both surprised to hear from him, but they were equally surprised with the news he shared. Both immediately expressed their desire to rush to their father's side. By the end of the call, they agreed to wait until their father was out of the hospital, saying they would be glad to make arrangements to come and help take care of him.

That night, Rich stayed at his father's house, the house they grew up in. Realizing how close he'd come to losing his dad, he decided to go through his father's files, knowing his father had legal documents in place to address his health and finances in the event of serious illness, injury, or... It would be nice to know where they were in the event they were necessary. As he thumbed through the files in his dad's bottom desk drawer, he came across an envelope that had his mother's name penned in the upper left corner, but it lacked a return address. His mouth dropped as he pulled out a very short handwritten note dated nearly thirty years before.

"It is better this way. Take care of the kids. Someday I hope they'll understand. I will always love them."

Seeing the words on the page started a flood of emotion. Memories washed over him as he recalled hearing the words from his dad who read it to them, all those years ago. Unable to sleep, Rich turned to his notebook and put his thoughts into lyrics…

RICH'S NOTEBOOK

Do we really know or understand
The power we all have in our hands
The answer's beyond a twist of fate
The question's not IF, but WHAT will we create

REFRAMING

In the **Rhythm of Reframing,**
we lead with gratitude, we accept the traumas of our
past without letting them limit us, we meet people
where they are, and honor feedback.

When we **Reframe,**
a new perspective emerges, and a shift happens!

9

GRATITUDE

Gratitude is the melody for the song of success.

Eight days passed before Rich was arranging his father's release from the hospital. It had been a trying week, as well as an emotional one. Every morning, Rich woke up with anxiety that would only be quelled after calling the nurse's station to hear how his father had been throughout the night. The news that he was stable always brought him a sigh of relief ... and it wasn't until he had that reassurance himself that he would provide his sister and brother with the daily update.

And he never missed a single opportunity to visit his father. He played guitar and read to his dad in the afternoons, which seemed a strange role reversal from when his dad read to them as kids.

Tim and Terri were very concerned, and he knew that their offer to fly in was sincere. Still, he assured them that he was fine and didn't need any help. Truth be told, if they did come, Rich had no idea how he would deal with them all being in one place. Now in his mid-40's, it had been years since they'd all been under one roof. He insisted that there was no reason for them to drop everything and rush to help, no reason at all.

And every time he repeated that, the twins would tell him how much they appreciated everything he was doing for their dad.

Although Rich assured them that they didn't need to come, Tim and Terri wouldn't take no for an answer and announced that they would be there before their dad was released from the hospital. They wanted to talk to the doctors with Rich and be there to help when their father went home.

"Rich, take the day off. We'll spend the day with him at the hospital today," they offered. "You need a break, and we want to make sure we understand what he needs now, too."

Their words were met with resistance. Rich still didn't want and resisted their offers to help. Rather than being grateful, he resented them for stepping in. Somehow, it brought up all the painful memories from their youth. His job was always being the big brother and protector.

In the end, the three of them went to the hospital together, and once again, Rich felt out of place in the presence of the twins.

His brother, Tim, had always been the sensitive one, and that hadn't changed. As he sat by his father's bedside and held his hand, he cried and expressed his regret for not being there when his dad needed him the most.

And Rich interjected, reminding Tim not to upset their father.

Terri, on the other hand, was busy taking notes and getting up to date on the doctor's instructions—what could he eat, what couldn't he eat, what was he allowed to do, what couldn't he do. The questions were endless.

Rich reminded her that he had already gone over all of that with the doctor, physical therapist, and dietitian. Quizzically, Terri stared at Rich and came right out and asked, "Did you write it all down?" Of course, the whole time she had been holding a small notebook marked "Dad's Healing Plan" on the cover. Inside, every detail was noted, which Rich secretly appreciated.

At the end of the day, their father, happy to see his three treasures together, said he was tired and insisted that they all go get something to eat. Just as Rich began to protest, feeling uneasy about spending any more time than necessary alone with the twins, they all agreed, saying that was a good idea.

It was Rich who broke the silence on the ride home, which was just a few short minutes from the hospital.

"I told you I have everything under control, and as you can see, there really isn't much you can do. There's no reason for you to stick around for another week or two," he said.

"Rich, we really appreciate everything you've done for Dad. We really do. I don't think you realize, though, how hard it is to take care of someone on a full-time basis. Dad is going to need a lot of care, and it isn't easy to do that alone. Why can't you accept our help? He's our father, too, and we are all responsible," Terri said.

"Maybe he doesn't trust us," Tim added.

"It's not that," Rich said. "Of course, I trust you."

"He's pushing us away, just like he used to," Tim said, again talking to Terri as if Rich wasn't in the car. "He still thinks of us as kids, and he knows what's best for all of us. We're grownups now and don't need protecting anymore, Rich!"

Terri carefully responded.

"Rich, we're not going anywhere. It might be best for all of us if you accept that and maybe try to be a little appreciative, too. We're doing this for Dad, and we're doing it for you, as well," she said.

Her words were met with silence.

When they got to their father's house, Rich pulled into the driveway to drop them off. He wanted nothing more than to go home and be alone. He certainly didn't want to listen to his brother and sister telling him how he should feel.

After having a quick bite to eat, he pulled out his guitar and strummed a few chords, hoping music would serve as a distraction, but it was one of the rare times that he couldn't get in the groove. Just as his mind was forming a rhythm, his thoughts would interrupt it, and he had to start over. Something was bothering him. Maybe it was Tim and Terri, but he'd always been able to handle them, so he told himself it had to be something else.

Was it his dad? He didn't think so ... his dad was on the upswing and in good hands. But something was nagging at him. It was the note their mom had left. *Just where was she?* He thought.

Deep in thought, it dawned on him that it wasn't the twins' fault that he wasn't close to them. Maybe it wouldn't have been that way if their situation had been different. When their mom left, the twins automatically turned to each other—after all, they had always been connected as twins. They shared space in the womb and shared a bedroom together! Rich was always the brother "in charge."

Suddenly, Rich wanted to know more, and he opened his laptop.

He logged in and began searching his mother's name on all social media platforms. He looked for relatives who might know where she had gone, but he didn't even find a mention of her associated with any of them.

Then he turned to Google, searching her maiden name and married name to no avail. It occurred to him that maybe she had remarried, and in that case, he might not ever be able to find her.

After clicking on many search results, he did find a link with her remarried name. The search had left him drained, and he decided to quit for the night, vowing to return to the search soon.

***

The next day, the threesome picked up their father and brought him home.

Terri posted the dietary guidelines on the refrigerator and got busy making a grocery list so she could prepare healthy meals for their dad, while Tim sent an update to their families back in Arizona. It had been years since they'd all been under the same roof, let alone in the house they grew up in together, and it made Rich uncomfortable. He wasn't used to anyone else intruding on his time with his father, even if it was his siblings.

And it showed. At one point, when they had been on each other's nerves too many times, Tim told Rich to stop being jealous. Then, Terri said he was ungrateful.

It was their father who put it to rest.

Tim and Terri had left to pick up a prescription and a few groceries, and Rich voluntarily stayed behind with his father, who was sitting in his recliner.

"What a blessing it is to have all my kids here," his dad said. "I'm a lucky man."

"I guess so, but I don't think we need them anymore. You and I can do this," Rich replied.

"You never were one to accept help, even when you were a boy," his dad said. "Oh no, you were always the one in charge. You wanted people to turn to you, not the other way around."

"Well, I was the oldest," Rich argued.

"That's one reason why I always worried most about you, son," his father confessed.

"You worried about *me?*" Rich couldn't hide the confusion or surprise in his voice.

"Sure, I did. You took it upon yourself to watch the twins, get them off to school, check homework, and tell them what to do, and they accepted that. They even learned to turn to you when they needed something. You became a surrogate parent, and it's partly on me that I let you step into this role. With your mom's mental health issues, our life was messy. I didn't worry about Tim and Terry because I knew you were at the ready if they needed anything at all, even if I was not available due to work. You, on the other hand, didn't turn to anyone. Even with lots of friends, you were always the one in charge. I guess you didn't always have someone you felt like you could turn to, did you?"

"Not true, I turned to you, and I came out all right," Rich said.

"In some ways, yes, you did," his father said.

"What do you mean ... in *some* ways?" he asked.

"Well, your brother and sister were just ten when your mom left suddenly, and I was overwhelmed with grief, fear, life and buried myself in my work," his father began.

With Rich's new knowledge about the note his mom had left, the mention of her caused him to twinge. He did not want to cause stress for his dad during this healing time!

"And it was only natural that they needed more care, so they learned how to accept and receive and trust. You helped them feel safe, Rich, and they learned how to be grateful because of it. They've told me many times how much they appreciate everything you did for them when they were kids," his dad said.

"They did? Why didn't they tell me that?" asked Rich.

"I think they have said it, and I'm saying it now. Yet you somehow can't hear it. I guess it's because you always felt responsible for their happiness and mine, so it just seemed to be part of your role. Your mom's departure was tough on all of us, but we never talked about it. We just moved on. It's a shame, really, because I can see that you're reluctant to accept support to this day," he said.

"I am not," Rich denied his father's words.

"Oh, yes, you are. There are times you don't accept help or feedback from me. You're often defensive. And you can't deny that you're not being very good at accepting help from your sister and brother. Talk about resistance! And when it comes to your music, you have to admit that it's not easy for you to accept help or feedback with your songs, either. Am I right?" his father asked.

Rich was happy to see that even though his dad's health had declined, he was as observant as ever. He didn't want to admit that he knew his dad was right, but he knew he couldn't deny it, either.

"Yes, you're right. I can see it now," he said as his father's words made him think about his reaction to Mindi's feedback and others more recently.

"Rich, put your pride or whatever it is aside and empower them to help. Think of it this way, their support will also give you more time for your songwriting! Besides, it'll improve your relationship with them significantly, if you let it. When you let yourself appreciate people and express gratitude, it's the best thing you can do for a relationship. It's a connection that brings relationships to the next level, son."

Humbled, Rich agreed.

"Even if I do accept their help and learn to appreciate it, it probably won't make a difference in our relationship. The damage is done," he said.

"Hogwash. All it takes is a little communication and a gratitude attitude to get everything going in the right direction, Rich. One of the best things you'll learn about gratitude is that it makes everything better. It turns criticism into feedback that you gladly accept and appreciate. I guess you can say it opens doors to a new perspective."

"What? Why?" Rich asked.

"Because once you exercise gratitude in everything you do, you'll find that you get even more of the very things you are grateful for. As those things come rolling into your life, good things happen; your relationship with yourself and your siblings improves. Your bank account increases. Your songs get better and get noticed. Your …"

"I get it; I get it, Dad," Rich laughed. "I promise I'll try."

"Don't try it. Do it. When you say 'try,' that gives you an out and shows you're not committed or leading with intention! Life's too short to go it alone. Collaboration is a gift that benefits all. You know that well from your music. Let your sister and brother be a part of your life and enjoy new growth!

"Like Tim and Terri, most people have nothing but the best intentions. A little appreciation takes very little effort, but it has more impact on you and the people in your life than anything else ever will … and that's what having a Gratitude Attitude can do," his father added.

As Rich listened to his father's words, he realized how much he depended on his wisdom and advice. And just how close he'd come to losing it. No doubt, Tim and Terri felt the same.

"Thank you, Dad. I needed to hear that. And…" he said, before his voice broke.

"And what?"

"And I'm grateful for every day with you. I hope that means I'll get many more," Rich finished as tears welled in his eyes.

"Me, too, son. Me, too," his father replied before leaning back in his recliner. "Now, I think I hear the garage door opening. Why don't you go help your brother and sister while I take a nap? You three have a lot to catch up on, I think."

10

ACCEPTANCE

Accepting the unexpected expands our ability to shift.

I t wasn't easy for Mindi to accept her limitations. Years ago, before Rose was born, it was something she'd promised herself she would never do. She'd told herself that she'd never give someone else the power to control her life or threaten her wellbeing.

She'd learned her lesson the hard way, back when she was married to Rose's father, Shane. Theirs had been a whirlwind romance that had taken Mindi by surprise. For the first time, she'd let herself fall for someone, and she let her entire world revolve around him—to the point that the other relationships in her life began to suffer. What she had thought was love, however, turned into control. Her husband of two years was a sought after and very handsome session musician. He had increasingly become critical, demanding that she conform to his wishes. He said she spent too much time with her family and his—after all, she was married, and he was supposed to be the first priority in her life. In an attempt to appease and please him, her world increasingly shrank and revolved solely around him, to the point where she even shut out her friend, Jamie, and her parents.

At the time, Mindi's work was getting increasingly noticed. Her attention to detail and her professionalism as a concert producer were highly commended. More than once, she was offered an opportunity for advancement; however, her husband frowned upon her taking on additional responsibilities. On several occasions, he'd told her that her job was to be his wife, and he was not willing to make any sacrifices for the sake of her career.

Initially, Mindi was thrilled to be with someone who shared her love of music and was a notable in the music industry. She was also flattered that he loved her so much that he wanted her by his side all the time. He even showered her with gifts. He always said, "I need you," which warmed her heart and made her feel special … until his tone became angry, stifling, and overbearing. It was increasingly clear that they had not been in agreement about their expectations of each other and their marriage.

She began to feel like she wanted more than to be someone's wife. She wanted more than a dead-end job. When she expressed that to her husband, he voiced his anger and dug his heels in even deeper. Over time, it became a source of discontent between them, causing more than a few arguments that became increasingly heated. Whenever Mindi would ask that they talk things out, the opportunity would always be delayed by his work or her work or other "have to's."

There was a lot of avoidance going on, she thought. When therapy was raised as a possibility, her husband would say "maybe." And then he'd get angry when Mindi brought it up again.

Mindi didn't feel like there was anyone she could talk to. Shane wouldn't talk to her, and on the occasions when she spoke with her parents, it was strained since she didn't feel safe to share the details of what was going on in her marriage.

Then Mindi became pregnant, and she hoped that the news that they were starting a family would bring her and her husband together once again. Her husband had a different viewpoint, however. He became even more controlling, refusing to let her go places and demanding to know who she was talking to at all times. She was carrying his child, after all. He even demanded that she quit her job, insisting that she give up her career and become a stay-at-home mom. "No one needs you like me, and I want you at home and on my arm," he would scream.

A once confident and independent woman, Mindi became compliant—anything to keep the peace and avoid yet another argument—anything except resigning from her job. She didn't want to give up her job just yet, anyway. She'd worked too hard to get into the industry. She and her mentor had built a career path that she was committed to, and she found she enjoyed the challenges and excitement that her work brought into her life— not to mention the money that supported them whenever Shane's sessions slowed down for a month. Besides, it was a reprieve and a way to get away from the marriage that was becoming increasingly unhappy.

At work, Mindi became withdrawn and disconnected from her co-workers for fear they may "find out."

Rose's birth was a happy occasion. Mindi's and Shane's parents adored their granddaughter. Mindi loved every minute she spent with her while she was on maternity leave. And that made her husband happy, as well. He liked having his wife at home at all times, "where she was supposed to be."

During lunch one day at their favorite spot, Mindi mentioned that they were fortunate that her parents were willing to babysit Rose when she returned to work. The mere mention of her going back to work triggered her husband's anger, and for the first time in their relationship, his behavior frightened Mindi. She walked on eggshells, hoping to steer the conversation toward safer topics, but it was her husband who brought the subject up again.

It was late at night when he'd come home from going out with his buddies after a session, and he walked into the bedroom, ready to pick a fight. She knew the signs and saw what was coming ... but she was blindsided when he suddenly grabbed her by the arms, pulled her out of bed, and pushed her against the wall. As she fought back tears and tried to free herself from his grip, she was met with a harsh slap across the left side of her face.

Helpless against his height and power, Mindi promised to quit her job.

The next day, when her husband went to work, she searched for clarity and struggled with her love for him, but stronger still was the voice inside that wouldn't let her minimize what had happened. She knew in her gut that this was only the beginning of a harsh reality, and there was no way she would subject her child to that life. So, she packed their bags, scooped up Rose, and in tears knocked on the door of her childhood home, where safety was trusted.

The next day, Mindi filed a police report and got a restraining order against her husband. After taking a few days of sick leave to allow the bruising to subside, she attempted to cover the evidence of his abuse with makeup and returned to work. Receiving silent stares and questions of concern, she offered no explanation. Simply saying she had taken a fall, Mindi offered no additional information and stepped into business as usual mode. She didn't even tell anyone when she filed for divorce.

The nightmare continued for another six months as the police were called to her home and her office when her husband would show up, demanding to see her. The final divorce decree ended their contact with each other.

Mindi was in a constant state of sadness, anger, and embarrassment for subjecting herself and those around her to Shane's dysfunction. She hardened from this experience and started a new job with a clean slate, where her personal life wouldn't be the subject of whispered concern or pity among her coworkers. Mindi promised herself at that point that she would never let anyone have the power to control or hurt her again and that she would stand in her strength forever more.

The temporary limitations from losing her eyesight and breaking her collar bone left Mindi feeling vulnerable for the first time since then. Losing her independence and control over her life was more than uncomfortable. At the same time, she was grateful that it was not permanent and able to recognize that the situation could be a turning point in her life.

Her recovery was going well, and Mindi heeded the advice of both her doctors and parents and took a break from traveling for a couple months. However, she did go to the office a few times a week to work on the next series of concerts. This slower pace, being off the road and home with family for more than 10 days a month, offered Mindi time for rest and play (especially with Rose), and reflection, all things that seemed to be more of a commodity during the past years.

Since she was restricted from driving, her father drove her to and from the office. While he was adamant about her not taking a car service, Mindi was increasingly apologetic for the inconvenience.

On the drive to work one morning, Mindi and her dad were talking. "I'm so grateful to you and Mom, and I wish I didn't have to impose on you anymore, Dad. You know how much I hate not being able to do what I need to do on my own," Mindi said.

"Oh, I know that well, Mindi," he replied.

"Dad, I've also learned that there are times when we get to accept the fact that there are things that are beyond our control, and I've found that we can always learn from them," she shared.

"Exactly," her dad replied. "It might do you some good to look at your circumstances differently—this is something you get to do to heal inside and out. You owe that to yourself ... and to Rose. Take this as a sign that change in your life is inevitable."

I don't ever want to be a burden, and I can't stand not being able to do everything I need to do at home or at work. I am learning, though, to accept where I am and the support that is authentically offered."

"Well, that's huge progress! Tell me, Mindi, do you still love your job, I mean really love it? Like you can't wait to get up and go to work every day?" he asked with genuine curiosity.

"Sure, I do," she answered without a hint of hesitation. The last time she was asked this question by her friend, Jamie, her reply was sincere when she said, "Yes." This time, though, when she heard herself, she wondered who she was trying to convince, her dad or herself?

The truth was that Mindi did have her own doubts. It all started when she'd been home recovering for a month and returned to the office for the first time since suffering her illness. Everyone welcomed her back and expressed concern for her, but she noticed there was something lacking. The concern wasn't personal. It was polite and professional—something Mindi had always encouraged in the workplace, but for the first time, she found it to be superficial and lacking in compassion.

It occurred to her that she'd worked with her team for years, but they didn't really know her or vice versa. She had intentionally avoided personal conversations that revealed any details about her life away from the office. But now she noticed the relationships her coworkers had with each other, and that made her feel alone, even when she was among them.

She questioned herself. What if she had been wrong? What was the point of building a wall around herself when, in fact, they were all in it together on a mission to succeed. She'd built that wall to protect herself, but in doing so, had kept something more important out of her life—meaningful connected relationships and a sense of camaraderie.

And then she also realized that she wasn't indispensable. Not only was the company surviving fine without her, but she wondered if she was even missed.

For years, she'd told herself that she didn't need anyone or anything ... she could do it all. But now she wondered if it was worth the price she'd paid.

On the evening of the day she first returned to work, Mindi was disturbed by her revelation. Unable to sleep, she once again listened to her audiobook, *Universal Relationship Rhythms*. The book had become her go to, and like she had done several times, she fast forwarded to a particular section of interest. This time, she chose Reframing. The first time she'd listened to it, it hadn't hit home, but this time she grasped the meaning when the narrator talked about the need to reframe to reclaim what one wants. Her aha moment was that this was all happening for her, and an opportunity was presenting itself. She had a choice to make—to stay bold and cold or step into a thriving life with meaningful connections.

On her second week back, Mindi gathered her team in the large conference room. There were plenty of oohs and aahs as they marveled at the breakfast spread and beautifully wrapped gifts at each spot on the table. Inside was a hand-crafted microphone statue with a plaque at the base that was personalized to each team member and an inscription that read, "TEAM, It's a new day! With gratitude, Mindi."

She recognized each person for their contribution and support and thanked them for rising to the occasion in all ways, making sure they knew how much she appreciated them and was proud of them. It felt good to be able to give herself permission to commend her team, and they, too, shared their gratitude! The buzz around the office that afternoon was a far different energy than in the past, and it felt good to everyone!

It occurred to Mindi that her parents were right. She had gone to great lengths to protect herself from being hurt, to the extent that she hadn't allowed herself to entertain the possibility of being happy.

It was then that Mindi fully accepted the fact that the life she'd created might not be the one she really wanted for the long term. Her drive, persistence, grit, and know-how had served her well to this point, and it had helped her become a recognized and accomplished award-winning concert producer. But it wasn't enough now.

For the first time, she wanted more and trusted that it was

possible. There was just one problem: she wasn't clear about what she wanted … and she intended to find out.

11

PERSPECTIVE

A perspective stalled by the past
limits the present.

I'm so glad you're seeing things differently and gaining a new perspective. It's no secret that we've been really worried about you, Mindi," her mother said. "While we are proud of your accomplishments, it has saddened us that you are so driven and might not ever let yourself enjoy life or let love into your life. You know that the bond your father and I have and the love we have for you and Rose are the most important things in our lives. You deserve to have that in your life, too. It's good to be successful and independent, and those things are just a slice of your life and not enough," her mother said.

"I'm clear about that now," Mindi assured.

"Knowing that you're doing something that is meaningful and

that brings you joy is priceless. A paycheck can't give you that. And there's also the opportunity to know that you're making a difference in people's lives, whether it's within your own family, community, or in your career. That is one of the most rewarding feelings you can have. It's one reason why I volunteer at the women's shelter," her mom explained.

"Oh, I thought you did that because of what happened to me," Mindi replied.

"Initially, I did, and then I found that it made me feel good to know that I was helping others—that I could support women as they pick themselves up and make a fresh start," her mom shared.

"Well, Mom, I hate to say you're right," Mindi smiled, "but ... lately, I've been considering submitting my resignation. I guess you could say that by not being able to see well, I've suddenly started to see things much more clearly. It's occurred to me that there's something more out there for me—I just don't know yet what it is. I do know, though, that I haven't found it where I am."

"I'm really proud of you for considering what could be next, Mindi. That said, I can't tell you what that might be—only you can do that. But I do think it might help if you expose yourself to new experiences and people. Heaven knows, you're not going to find what's missing sitting here day after day," her mom said.

Then after a pause, she excitedly added, "Hey, I have an idea! If you're serious about resigning, let's take that road trip! Your father and I have been waiting until the time is right—we didn't want to leave you and Rose when you needed us. But if you're not working, it's the perfect opportunity for you and Rose to come with us! We'll have such fun, and it just might help you get clear on what you really want and create a new vision for your future."

After reviewing her finances over the next week and factoring in the bonus of nearly three months of accrued vacation time, Mindi took a giant leap into trust. The next week, she penned and submitted her resignation, while also recommending her replacement.

"Liz has proven herself and her value to the organization. Above all, she has built solid relationships that invite collaboration and cooperation within the team and those we serve. I highly recommend her as my replacement and know she will bring a fresh perspective to the role and the industry as a whole."

The surprise party they held for Mindi was warm, joyful, and emotional. She was acknowledged and celebrated by all. It was bittersweet as she was leaving behind a cohesive team and stepping into a new part of her journey.

Rich read in an online music trade magazine that Mindi had been recovering from an accident and had recently resigned her position. Concerned for her, he shot her a quick text. "Hi, Mindi, long time, no talk. Just saw your announcement—wishing you well!"

He did not receive a reply.

A few weeks later, Mindi and Rose began their cross-country trip with her parents in their new RV.

Seeing the sites from the road was a novelty for Mindi, who usually traveled from one airport to another. Her father wasn't one for interstates; he preferred to visit small towns, where he could explore historic landmarks and experience the local lifestyle and culture. It was both educational and enlightening. They were all having a blast—camping was new and fun!

They visited village festivals and celebrations and enjoyed the cuisines from across the cultures that U.S. towns offered at different stops along the way. It was a new perspective of a world that Mindi had always known was out there but had never paused to experience. Her former daily rush of hundreds of emails slowed to a mere few personal notes from colleagues, and there were no late-night calls. Mindi felt so free!

It was a visit to an Indian reservation in the Southwest that had a profound impact on her. After a guided tour, they were invited to view the impressive handicrafts, ceramics, and carvings made by the community artisans, ranging in age from eight to ninety. As a special treat, they witnessed the culture exhibited by traditional native music, dances, and ceremonial rituals. The music drew her in with its story and emotion that was exemplified by a message she saw on the wall: "We are all connected as humans first, and music is our great uniter."

What struck Mindi was how music is universal and so much more than entertainment. To the Native American community, it was powerful and spiritual and a way to communicate their customs and beliefs. This music had meaning and a purpose. It represented life and the relationships that they held in high value.

Connecting in this way, Mindi found the experience inspirational, and she wondered … *What if we could truly connect humanity through music!* She also wondered what it would be like if we used music to bring people together, shed light on issues, and promote a better world.

Having been involved in a couple benefit concerts over the years, Mindi's mind was spinning.

What if she started her own music promotion company, one that featured artists, songs, and causes that would have a positive impact on the world? At first, she shrugged it off, thinking she was crazy to dive back in again. But she kept being called back to the idea, even telling her parents, "Why not now? I know what I'm doing!

Suddenly, Mindi knew exactly what she wanted to do. The answer had always been in music, but the heart-driven purpose and meaning had never been there. Now that she'd found a way to create that meaning, she felt empowered and motivated to make it happen and knew she was up to the challenge!

First, she needed to envision the business and what it would bring to the industry and those who would benefit. Second, she knew it would never get off the ground without a business plan, funding, and she'd need a killer team—one that was on board with her vision with the relationships and contacts to make it happen.

***

In the meantime, Rich was in Arizona, where he was helping his father settle in at his sister's house. It was a permanent move that the entire family agreed on, and he wouldn't let his father make it without him. More than anything, he wanted to make sure his father had the best care he could get, and while he knew Terri loved their dad, he couldn't help but feel the need to be needed, as well.

Rich initially had reservations about spending a lot of time with the twins. For years, their communications had been limited to impersonal "happy birthdays" and the regular inquiry into how their father was doing and whether he needed anything. As an uncle, though, Rich had always remembered Terri's children on their birthdays and holidays, making sure he sent a card with an amount of money equivalent to their birthday age, plus five dollars for good luck. It was easier than buying a gift, given he had never spent an extensive amount of time with them and didn't know a great deal about them. The kids, though, were fond of "Uncle Rich" and enjoyed getting a special present from him and the postcards they received from his travels.

So, while Rich's reasons for going to Arizona stemmed around his father, he also found he enjoyed the chance to get to know his niece and nephew better. Unlike his relationship with Tim and Terri, his relationship with them wasn't stilted and weighted by their past. It was simply a time to get to know each other, whether they were being silly, playing catch, or asking Uncle Rich to tuck them into bed at night.

Terri even commended him for his connection with her kids.

"Rich, it's nice having you around. I know the kids are really enjoying spending time with you," she said.

"I'm enjoying them, too. They're great," Rich acknowledged.

"What happened?" she asked. "Why did we drift apart?"

Taken aback by the question, Rich paused before answering, even though he was more open now to talking than he had been when they were first dealing with their dad's heart attack months prior.

"I don't know. I guess when we were younger, it was the age gap. And then you and Tim always had each other—I was just the big brother who wanted to be there for you. Then you went off to college together, and we started to lose touch," he said, shrugging his shoulders.

"I hear you," Terri said. "Maybe this is a chance for us to start over."

While Rich found it difficult to step back and let his siblings step up and take care of their dad, he owed it to his dad and himself to make an effort. And he had to admit, Tim and Terri were pretty cool and very welcoming, and his dad loved Arizona and being with his grandchildren.

One day, his siblings surprised him by asking him to play some songs for the kids.

"Did you know your Uncle Rich is a musician? He writes his own songs. Maybe he'll play some of them for you," Tim said.

"Nah, you guys don't want to listen to me sing," Rich argued.

"Yes, we do!" Terri exclaimed. "As I recall, you're pretty good— which brings me to ask, what's the latest with your songwriting?"

"I am—well, I was writing," Rich corrected himself. "But then Dad got sick, and…"

"Hey, isn't it true that some of the best songs are based on some of the toughest, most emotional experiences? This might be a great time for you to write a new song," Tim said.

Tim's partner, Oscar, then spoke up.

"Wait a minute! There's a festival this weekend, and they're having an open mic night. Why don't you play, Rich? We'll all come and cheer you on!" he said.

For some reason, Rich was reluctant to play in front of his family. His father had always been safe—but he didn't want to put himself in a position to be judged by the twins. In his mind, it was better to be safe than sorry.

"Thanks, but I don't think so," he said. "I'll pass."

"C'mon, it'll be fun!" Terri argued. "And don't worry about Dad. He's doing great, and it would do him a world of good to get out, even for a short time. Think of it this way, Rich, you'd be doing Dad a favor."

"I'd like that," his dad said. "Terri's right. A little fresh air might be nice, and a family outing, well, that would be even better."

It was an unexpected perspective, but one that Rich couldn't argue. He'd do anything for his dad, and his dad knew it.

To Rich's pleasant surprise, the open mic night was a big success for him. Something was different in this audience and with this performance than all the other open mic nights or paid gigs he'd done previously. Rich could feel that his lyrics and music reached the people in the audience.

When they returned home, his siblings showered him with encouragement.

"You're really good, Rich. What are you doing still selling stocks?" Tim asked.

"He's right," Terri chimed in. "You are talented. If you really invested some time into it, I think you could go places."

"I've been working on it," Rich admitted. "I might be good, but I'm just not good enough, not yet."

"Hmmm, that did not seem to be the case tonight!" Terri attested.

***

A couple weeks later, Terri sat him down to talk.

"Rich, I enjoy having you here, but you don't need to stay. The doctor said Dad is doing well, and I promise that we'll take good care of him. Why don't you go write songs and find whatever it is that's missing in your life and your music?" she asked.

"What makes you think something is missing from my life?" he shot back.

"I've always just had a feeling that there's something you're searching for. I'm not sure what it is, but something tells me you won't be happy until you find it," she said.

Surprised at his sister's insightfulness, he thought of their mother.

That night after everyone had gone to bed, now knowing his mother's remarried name, Rich opened his laptop and renewed his search. This time, it wasn't long before his search led him to their mother's online obituary. Stunned as he read it, he realized that she had been deceased for many years. For decades, he had resented her for not being in his family's life, but now he understood that she couldn't have been. It put things into a different perspective.

The next morning, he brought the printed obituary to breakfast. It was time to bring everything to light. By this time, he had shared that he found the letter with his dad and that she had passed away, which he had not been aware of. His dad had told him that not searching for his wife was very hard, but in the long run, he knew it would be best for all of them. Up to this point, Rich was not sure how to broach the sensitive subject with his siblings.

Now that he was mending his relationship with them, it was time to mend his lack of emotional relationship—with his mother. As he sat down to think about this, a few lines came to him out of the blue…

RICH'S NOTEBOOK

Each of us a star, a brilliant light
Every star illuminates the night in its own way
All the stars combine to make the day

RESILIENCE

In the **Rhythm of Resilience,**
we stand up and step forward with consistent action
and accept support to courageously face
and navigate inevitable change.

When we are **Resilient,**
our relationships are inspired
and renewed!

12

CONSISTENCY

Consistent action is the kryptonite of complacency.

With his family's encouragement, Rich returned to songwriting with a renewed vigor. This time, however, his songs came from a place of peace and acceptance, from his heart. Having learned of his mother's passing and later discovering that she suffered from severe depression, he and his brother, sister, and dad were able to let go of the guilt and resentment that had haunted each of them since her abrupt departure from their family. In addition, Rich developed an even deeper respect for his father, who he learned had also been waiting for answers and blaming himself for his wife's departure. Until now, this was a topic that was never addressed.

When the family finally sat down to disclose and discuss their past, they each learned a great deal about the other—things they had never shared. The old feelings of abandonment and disconnection they carried in their minds had impacted them individually and as a family throughout the years. And with that knowledge came understanding and compassion. In the present, releasing the past had brought them closer, and they felt free to share and validate their once hidden feelings and fears.

It was enlightening.

In the end, it was their father who encouraged them to let go of the past and move forward.

"There are things we can never change, but the one thing we can change is how we respond and how we let it affect us. I've learned that life is short, and that means that we all get to live every minute of it to the fullest. And that's what I want for all of you, too. Do what makes you happy. Make your mark, and create your legacy," he said.

Along with the encouragement of his siblings, those words were the inspiration and kick in the pants that Rich needed to take action and pursue his songwriting journey. During his last week in Arizona, he decided to attend an entrepreneurial workshop by a well-known expert in the industry—one whom he had admired and respected for quite some time. Initially, his interest stemmed from the desire to enhance his expertise in his career and make his services more desirable to prospective entrepreneurial clients. Although he was set financially, his interest was specifically in creating more passive income and protecting his intellectual property, his songs. These were big things he wanted to understand more fully. He wanted to have his ducks in a row before sidelining his current business and diving full time into his music.

On the day of the event, he walked into the already half-full ballroom. After signing in at the registration desk and receiving his packet of materials, his eyes passed across the room, looking for a table that wasn't taken. He stopped when he recognized what looked like a familiar face. Just as he was peering closer, thinking it couldn't possibly be her, she turned her head and caught his eye.

He knew then that it was, without a doubt, Mindi.

Sensing that they were both initially hesitant, he crossed the room and broke the ice.

"Hello, Mindi. What a pleasant surprise! I must say, though, that I didn't expect to see you here, of all places," he said.

"Hi, Rich," she returned his greeting. "You're so right. We're not exactly in LA, are we?"

"No, we're not," he laughed. "But it's good to see someone I know. I always hate being the odd man out at these things."

"Me, too," Mindi said. So, tell me, what brings you here? I mean, with your experience as a stockbroker and all. I would think it would be more likely to see you in Nashville or…"

"Actually, I've been on a writing spree, and I was in Nashville earlier this year. I registered for this workshop a while back. Actually, one of the reasons I'm here is to learn how I can afford to be a starving songwriter," he laughed. "How about you? How are you feeling since your accident? What brings you to Scottsdale?"

"I'm good now, feeling great. Amazing what forced rest will do for you!" she chuckled. "I chose to take a hiatus, and I'm taking a little time off to do some traveling with my daughter and parents. I recently saw a promotion for this event and thought I'd check it out," she said.

The two sat at a table and caught up, each treading very gently, careful not to bring up their last encounter. It was Mindi who broke the ice.

"So, how's your writing coming along?" she asked.

"Well, I took a break for a bit when my dad got sick, and now that he's doing better, I've decided to go for it! How about you? What's happening in your world, besides traveling?"

"I'm toying around with starting my own company or maybe a foundation, something that is heart centered and cause related. It's just in the idea stage, so there's not much to share. I thought this workshop might give me some insight that would help me get it off the ground," Mindi said. "While I have experience managing a company, I don't know all the ins and outs of owning one."

Their conversation ended when a gentleman stepped up to the microphone and delivered the opening address and introduction to their featured speaker, who told her story and shared the pillars for success. One message that was clear was the importance of consistency in building wealth and managing a business, using systems, tools, and processes. From that moment on, Rich and Mindi devoted their full attention to the information that was shared, each benefiting in different ways.

Rich and Mindi hung out over lunch, and at the conclusion of the event, Rich thanked Mindi for her company.

"I've enjoyed seeing you. And I want to apologize for my behavior the last time we talked. It was unforgiveable, and I regret it. It's good to see that you don't hold grudges," he grinned.

"It's all right. Actually, it's been great to connect here. I enjoyed it. I have to admit that I came across a little harsh myself, and I'm sorry if I offended you in any way. I really am. I hope you didn't let anything I said discourage you, Rich. Like I said back then, I've been impressed with some of your songs. I really have," she replied. "Oh, also, thanks for reaching out when you saw the article. Truth be told, I was not ready to connect with anyone at that point."

"No offense taken. As a matter of fact, your feedback actually ended up being very helpful. You might be surprised to find that I took it to heart and put it to good use. At least I think so," he said. "So, if it's okay with you, how about we let the past stay in the past and focus on today?"

"Agreed! In that case, I wouldn't mind listening to another song—if you don't mind, that is. I promise not to tear you down this time," she offered.

"You know what? I think I'd like that. Here," Rich said, passing her his business card. "Just scan that, and it'll take you to the updated catalogue of my songs. I suggest you listen to a few of the most recent ones. And I don't even expect a response—that way nobody's feelings get hurt."

"Thanks, Rich. I promise to take the time to listen to them. Actually, I'm looking forward to it."

***

Later that night, after listening to three of Rich's new songs, Mindi started writing a text to him, then stopped herself and dialed his number.

"Hello," he answered.

"Wow. Just wow," Mindi said. "Rich, these are good. I mean really good. They touched me, and that isn't always easy to do."

"You like them?" he asked, holding his breath.

"Like them? I love them! I can feel your passion in the lyrics. It's like every line leads to a stronger line that pulls the listener in even more," she told him.

"I appreciate that. Over the course of the last year, I've learned a lot. I learned that being a songwriter takes consistency and creating a relationship with my songs; you have to work on each song over and over until you get it right. Then you have to start all over with the next song," he shared. "My dad says that success takes consistent empowered action. I guess he's right. It's funny—looking back to some of my very first songs, I thought they were good—really good. Oh, did I have a lot to learn. I know now that writing songs is like anything else in the world—the more you do it, the better you get … and the more you want to be better at your trade."

"I think it's paying off for you, and that's a great thing. Tell me, have you sent these to your publisher?" she asked.

"Not yet. I want to make sure they're ready. I'd rather work on them until I know they're the best they can be before I put them out there," he said.

"I think they're close. As a songwriter, you've really grown. Your songs are meaningful, even unforgettable," she said.

"That means a lot to me, Mindi."

"I'd like to hear what your publisher thinks, when you are ready, that is. And, if you come up with anything new and want an objective opinion, please feel free to reach out to me. I want to continue to keep my thumb on the pulse of the business and listening to artists and songwriters like you will help me do that. I might not be producing concerts at the moment, but my new venture might offer some possibilities. In this industry, you can't walk away for too long. I know I have to stay relevant and, like you said, consistent."

"I just might take you up on that offer," Rich informed her.

"Great. Who knows? Maybe one day we'll be doing something entirely different, but something tells me that we're both on an exciting new path and we should keep going and see what happens. I've always loved the industry, and I'm curious where it'll take me from here, and I have a feeling that you'll be going places, too," she said. "Keep doing what you're doing, because it's made a difference. Like your dad said, take consistent empowered action. He sounds like a wise man!"

13

INSPIRATION

Inspiration is the power tool of creative vision.

Mindi's feedback gave Rich the inspiration he needed to improve his songwriting skills. In doing so, he discovered a lot about his previous efforts—and himself. Suddenly, he could listen to his songs objectively and was able to see them in a different light. As a published songwriter, he was validated, knowing that he had what it takes to write a hit song. But he now knew that there was more to songwriting than following the mechanics—for years, he'd been writing songs that were safe and that he thought would appeal to a large audience. However, safe meant generic. He hadn't gone out on a limb and risked baring his heart and soul in his songs—he hadn't created a relationship with his songs or with his listeners.

In an impromptu visit to a local bookstore, he got sidetracked by watching the other patrons in the store. He found himself imagining their stories and backgrounds, their joys and struggles—all things that make for great songwriting—and he was inspired to jot down some of his thoughts. Looking around for a piece of paper, he spied one sitting on an empty table nearby. Picking it up, he discovered that he was holding a vocabulary list in his hand. At the top of the page, the following words were printed:

Week 12 Vocabulary Words: Mrs. King's Class

A quick glance through a child's forgotten vocabulary list told him that all of the words started with the letter R. Curious, he skimmed through them.

Rapport	Relationship
Respect	Represent
Responsibility	Resistance
Reframe	Record
Resilience	Rhythm

Strange, he thought, every one of these words could apply to me. They've all come into play in my life in the past year. Taking another look, he read the definitions, and the one that resonated with him the most was resilience.

Re·sil·ience

the capacity to recover quickly from difficulties; toughness

It occurred to Rich that resilience was definitely something that would have benefited him years before. Rather than developing that capacity to bounce back, though, he had been unwilling to let his difficulties go, hanging onto them and allowing them to hold him back. Instead of being resilient, he'd let his disappointments and difficulties carry too much weight, ultimately, making him unable to move forward—until recently, that is. This was now his moment to face it. It was his time to stand up, step forward, and not be afraid to ask for support.

He was proud of how much he'd grown, as a person and as a songwriter. He'd made peace with his past and forged a new relationship with his sister and brother. Rich also had deepened his relationship with his father, and while he found that their roles had changed due to his dad's illness, he knew he'd never again take his dad or his siblings for granted. While he was grateful for that, he regretted that he nearly lost his father before coming to that realization.

His resilience as a songwriter was even more profound. Over the course of the last year, he had become keenly aware of one of his greatest pitfalls—his ego. In the past, he'd always wanted to be a hit songwriter, not because he wanted to change the world through the music he created, but because his ego craved the recognition and accolades of reaching that pinnacle of success. He had been striving to gain a feather in his cap, but he was going about earning it in the wrong way. His resistance to change had been his pitfall, for sure.

And it showed in the songs he'd written throughout the years. Revisiting them, it was apparent that, while he knew the mechanics of creating a rhythm, his music and lyrics had been out of sync with each other. If the lyrics were strong, he made the melody even stronger. The end result was like two people having an argument—with each person's voice rising in response to the other. In the end, they fought, instead of enhancing, each other. He knew now that the two didn't have to be equal, as long as they supported each other. A strong lyric could ride on a subtle melody, and an amazing melody didn't require overpowering lyrics.

His knee-jerk response to Mindi's feedback the year before was the perfect example, proof that he'd been out of sync and out of rhythm with everything he'd wanted to accomplish and become all along.

***

Hundreds of miles away, Mindi was discovering a different passion for her career, one that kept pulling her in an unexplored direction. She was coming to terms with the fact that the frequent travelling she'd been doing had not only caused her a great deal of stress, but it had also impacted Rose, who was truly enjoying her mother's full-time attention. While Mindi also intended to enjoy their time together, she knew it was temporary. She'd always prided herself on being able to support her family, and she knew she didn't want that to change. At the same time, she also knew that change is inevitable.

What if there were a way for her to do what she loved without all of the traveling? Something that could keep her closer to Rose, while staying in the entertainment industry that she loved? It occurred to her that she could outsource her services, picking and choosing select concerts, but that just seemed to be a watered-down version of what she'd always done. So, she kept her eyes and ears open, knowing that there had to be something out there that would allow her to do the things she wanted on her own terms.

It was during a visit to a renowned eye specialist in Denver that she received her inspiration. Not having visited this specialist before, she had Googled Dr. Linda Patel's practice. The ophthalmologist had impressive credentials, but what stuck out to Mindi was that she had founded a not-for-profit organization, consisting of a group of her peers who volunteered to treat indigent patients with sight-threatening diseases at no cost.

Sitting in the waiting room, she eyed a brochure promoting the organization. The company, "Healing Vision," had initially started on a small scale, treating the residents of an Indian reservation, but throughout the years, it had expanded to the underserved across the country and into some of the poorest nations. Over time, hundreds, maybe thousands, of optometrists had joined the cause, expanding their services to include prescription eyeglasses for military veterans.

And I have spent my career helping affluent musicians and people who can afford to pay top dollar for concert tickets, she thought. Somehow, her career no longer felt so fulfilling. In many ways, it paled in comparison to the real difference these people were making. A quick search on the web revealed a recent study that found that 88% of people worldwide ranked "vision" as the most valuable of their senses. *Hmmm…*, Mindi thought.

"Based on your records, I'm happy to say that I see significant improvement in your vision. However, there will be a possibility of a recurrence, especially for the next year. Your medications will help, but it is important to avoid situations or circumstances that are known to trigger your condition," Dr. Patel advised.

After agreeing to follow her recommendations, Mindi couldn't help but mention her not-for-profit organization.

"So many people see a need, but don't do anything about it. What inspired you?" she asked.

"Like you said, I saw a need. When I went into this profession, I did it because I wanted to help people. I wanted to improve their lives. If I could do that, I would know that I made a difference. Along the way, though, it became evident that the system only allowed me to help *some* people, and they usually weren't the ones who needed help the most. I had a vision to help people outside of the system, and after spending a decade talking about it, I finally did something. That's when Healing Vision was born," she answered.

"That's remarkable, and I'm sure it's extremely rewarding. It makes me wish I had chosen a career where I could have made a difference in people's lives. Promoting and managing sold-out concerts doesn't sound very impressive in comparison, does it?"

"My career revolves around vision, Mindi, but I've learned that it is also about observation, something I call our second sight. Observation is free, and everyone can access it. You have the gift of observation—use it to create your own vision. It happens when we are present and curious. If you look hard enough, I believe you'll find that, no matter what you do, you can use it to make a difference, too. I heal my patients through science—who knows, maybe you can find a way to heal people through music," Dr. Patel smiled.

***

The doctor's words weren't soon forgotten. As a matter of fact, her parting words never left Mindi's mind. As she replayed them in her head, she became more and more inspired.

"Maybe you can find a way to heal people through music."

Suddenly, inspiration gave way to an idea, and Mindi smiled.

"Maybe I can. Maybe I can," she said.

14

CHANGE

Renewal is unplugging from your past
to energize your future.

A few weeks later, after putting Rose to bed for the night, Mindi found that she was too restless to sleep, something she'd been experiencing with more frequency as time went on. When she worked long hours, that hadn't been the case. In those days, she was exhausted at the end of the day, but since she'd left her job, she found she had too much pent-up energy when the day was done to drift off to sleep quickly.

Rather than tossing and turning, she put her earbuds in to listen to an audiobook, a practice that she'd started when she needed to rest her eyes. Over time, she found she enjoyed listening to books as much as reading them. Flipping through the library of audiobooks saved on her phone, she settled on one of the favorites she was sometimes compelled to listen to again. Whenever she revisited *The Universal Relationship Rhythms,* she found that there was some nugget that she'd overlooked. To her surprise, it was also something that she needed to hear at that specific time, a coincidence she couldn't deny.

It was a bestselling book for a reason—the authors had pulled together some profound life principles and revealed that every area of life required rhythm in order to thrive. There were chapters that discussed the relationships people have with others, such as family members, friends, and coworkers, and the relationships they have with their career, their health, their finances, and even the environment. Even more important was the relationship people have with themselves. Like the book said, if one is out of rhythm in any area of their life, it will affect all areas of their life.

And that's precisely what had happened when she lost her vision. Her home life was out of rhythm with her work life. Her professional life was way out of rhythm with her non-existent personal life, and the rhythm was thrown so far off that each nut and bolt that had held her life together came loose.

On this night, she turned to the end of the book and the section entitled "Renewal," and she felt like the words were being spoken directly to her.

"Life is a series of endings and beginnings. There is a tendency to get so lost in the past that it becomes impossible to envision a brighter future. Rather than mourn or regret what once was, look upon the past as a period of growth. Like the passing seasons, change is inevitable. Embrace the changes before you and look to them as a time of renewal. This is an opportunity for every area of your life to sync together in perfect rhythm, while creating harmony in your relationship to yourself and the world around you."

That was precisely where Mindi felt she was in her life. She needed to step out of her comfort zone and make a decision about how to move forward, but unlike she'd done in the past, this time she knew the importance of strengthening relationships in all areas of her life, instead of avoiding them. On one hand, it was a scary proposition. On the other, though, it was exciting to consider what could be.

The entertainment industry is what she knew best, and she felt she had a strong professional relationship with the industry as a whole, even though she'd avoided establishing personal relationships within it. Like Dr. Patel had said, every career and industry provided an opportunity to make a difference, and Mindi was beginning to believe that. After all, music was a universal language! It was so much more than filling concert halls and stadiums. She'd had seen and experienced one aspect of music in the past, but she knew it held untouched potential she'd never before considered.

Knowing this was her season of renewal, Mindi had a dream to create a concert that would make all the concerts she'd promoted pale in comparison. It would be a concert that would relate to the people and the causes, hopes, and dreams that were important to them. It would promote a message that would benefit people from all walks of life and, even more, give back to them by raising funds to fight hunger and abuse, support wellness and mental health, and the many other causes and missions that impact people's lives.

She knew the vision for her business required widespread collaboration, input, and assistance. There were many spinning wheels that had to be set into motion—publishers, agents, and artists were just the tip of the iceberg. Based on her business experience as a concert producer, she knew she'd be doomed to failure if she went into this venture in a business-as-usual mode. For the first time, she was more prepared to relinquish some of her control, delegate responsibilities, and rely on a large network of people to connect and collaborate to bring it all together.

Rich was also at a crossroads. While being a stockbroker provided him with financial security and the flexibility to enjoy songwriting, travel, and his family, it wasn't his passion. He didn't relate to his career, not in the same way that he related to his songs. And as he became a more observant songwriter, he was able to inject more of his emotions into his music.

Like Mindi, he was entertaining doing something different with his life. Every time he considered his options, it was music that called his name. It made sense to Rich—after all, his relationship with music was the only one he had held dear, outside of his relationship with his father and now his siblings.

Yet he wondered why he was being pulled in a different direction. Yes, he'd grown as a songwriter, and he'd stood in his responsibility to repair the frayed relationships with his brother and sister, but he couldn't help but feel there was something more purposeful calling him.

Then it hit him. It was his mother. Her absence in his life had left him reluctant to get close to people for fear that they, too, would one day be gone, leaving him alone, confused, feeling abandoned and unable to move on. But now that he knew that he had answers, Rich found he was able to unplug from the past, let others in, and begin to see possibilities for the future. He could accept criticism, not taking it personally, and most of all, without believing that critical feedback meant someone didn't like him and cause them to walk out of his life, like his mom had done decades before.

That's why Rich's motives had always been ego driven; he hadn't received the approval and praise from his mother that he longed for. To compensate, his ego needed reinforcement and validation that he was worthy, that his songs were worthy.

He was visiting his dad at Terri's house when he received an unexpected phone call from Mindi on a Sunday morning. Actually, he was standing at the sink, helping his sister rinse breakfast dishes when the call came in. Seeing her name on the screen, he looked at his sister and said, "Hey, sorry, Ter, mind if I take this? It's Mindi."

"Oh, I get it—payback for all those years you helped Dad do the dishes, while Tim and I got to watch TV," she playfully replied, pretending to snap a dish towel in his direction.

"You got it, sis. Have fun," Rich grinned, walking away, phone in hand.

"Hi, Mindi," he answered cheerfully.

"Hi, Rich. Is this a bad time?" she asked.

"No, actually it's a great time," he smiled to himself as he recalled his exchange with his sister. "What's up?"

"Well, I had a business idea, and I thought I'd reach out. Rich, do you remember in the entrepreneurial workshop we both attended when they touched on not-for-profits?"

"I sure do. As a matter of fact, I still have the materials they gave us," he replied.

"I have to admit that I didn't pay close attention to some parts because they didn't pertain to me at the time," Mindi advised.

"They did discuss different types of businesses, like LLCs and nonprofit organizations. What is it you want to know?" he asked.

At first, Mindi hesitated to share her idea with Rich. Then, she once again felt a strong sense of the trust that they had established at the workshop. Knowing it was impossible to get the assistance she wanted without fully disclosing her idea, she leaned into that trust and told him all about her vision. When she finished, Rich seemed to love the idea just as much as she did.

"What an awesome idea! Oh, Mindi, this could be big!" he exclaimed. "Think of the big names you could get on board. I mean, you do have the connections, and if you can get some of the top artists and bands on board, there's no telling how big this could be."

"I wish I had your confidence, Rich; there are just so many moving pieces. I've never owned a business, and in the past, I've always been focused on producing for profits. This is foreign territory, and I'm going to need a lot of advice and help to make it happen," she said.

"Mindi, this is a bold vision, and it will happen. I'll be happy to introduce you to some people who have expertise in business who would be happy to assist," he offered.

Before their call ended, Rich offered Mindi an invitation.

"Mindi, I'm working on new song ... wanna hear it?"

"Absolutely," Mindi exclaimed.

Rich began reading in rhythm...

Each of us can stand for something good
Every time we rise, we elevate the place we live
We expand our souls by what we give
Tomorrow is not up to someone else
The hope you have is hope that you can trust
The truth is that the future is up to each of us

Each of us can build
Each of us can teach
And reach inside, we can guide
And what we leave is up to each of us

"Wow, Rich, that is so powerful. It correlates perfectly with what we've been talking about! Your words couldn't have come at a better time," Mindi said, a happy tear welling in the corner of her eye.

Looking back to when their journey started, this was a real turning point in their relationship as friends. When Mindi approached Rich with her idea, she believed he had something to contribute, but at the time, she didn't know just how valuable his assistance would be. Since they had reconnected at the workshop, she'd reached out to him several times when she had a thought or an idea, and she found that they were often on the same page. Even when they weren't, they responded with respect and went to work to reframe the approach for a new solution.

With the exception of her parents and best friend, Jamie, Mindi didn't have much experience with that type of personal relationship—one that was mutually beneficial based on respect and responsibility, and one where both parties were equally inspired to achieve a common goal.

And that inspired Mindi to discover the depths of what one executive producer and one songwriter could create together.

If anyone had told her the year before that she would be at risk of losing her vision, leave her job, and be working alongside Rich, she would have told them they were crazy. Yet here she was—a single mother without a job, boldly starting a venture with someone who had been at total odds with her not too long before.

Maybe it was crazy … but it was also inspiring. If they could make this dream a reality, they would not only be able to make a positive impact on the lives of many, but they'd alter their lives and relationship forever.

Like the book had told her, there is a rhythm to relationships. They have their ups and downs. There is a hook that pulls them together, and a harmony that lets them express their individuality without breaking their bond. And there is always a bridge, the chords that carry them from one stage to another.

It all made sense now, and she could see clearly how she had pushed such relationships away, fearing that letting anyone in would make her vulnerable to the pain she'd experienced in her marriage. The realization was like a new beginning, knowing that she didn't always have to have all the answers. She didn't have to always be the strong one. She could give herself permission to *feel*—and that was one of the most transformational thoughts she'd had in years.

Renewal and rhythms, she thought, was what she wanted her company to be about. Using music to inspire others to feel, to contribute, to make a difference in a world where she knew she had once been guilty of indifference. It would be about new beginnings in friendships, families, communities, and she even dared to think, the world.

It was with those thoughts that the name of her not-for-profit company was born.

The *R*Factor: The Universal Rhythms of Life

15

VISION

We are all connected as humans first,
and that's where the bottom line begins.

The sold-out concert was set against the magnificent sandstone that comprised the red-rock formations surrounding the natural amphitheater just outside Denver. Although Mindi was no stranger to Red Rocks Park and Amphitheatre, on this night, it took her breath away. So much planning and preparation had gone into manifesting her vision, and Mindi's mind was telling her that her company's success or failure would be determined tonight.

Standing in the wings, awaiting the moment Mindi would introduce the concert, Rich sensed her anxiety, and he took Mindi's hand to give it an encouraging squeeze.

"It's going to be great. How can it not be? After all, you've got the best production company and concert team … all trained by you! And look at the bands on board. How you managed to get some of the biggest names to perform for free I'll never know!" he said.

"One of my biggest ahas in bringing this vision to life is understanding that the power of connected relationships is a significant asset," Mindi admitted. "I am so grateful that *our* relationship has evolved, Rich. I couldn't have done this without you, and I can't begin to thank you enough."

"Oh, yes you can. As a matter of fact, you already have," he replied.

"I can't wait to hear your song performed against these acoustics, Rich. And I didn't do anything, really. There are many artists who have expressed interest in recording your song. 'Each of Us' is so cool that all the bands on the ticket will be performing it together tonight! Now, that's amazing!"

That was a point Rich couldn't argue. It was a milestone beyond his wildest imagination. For a brief moment, he allowed his pride and ego to celebrate his success, but it was passing. While he believed in this song like no other, his intentions were no longer about climbing to the top of the charts. Instead, he had a larger dream. Rich's vision was now to use his songs to spread a universal message of hope and healing, a message that every voice and every dream could be possible if we realize that we are all connected as humans on this planet we call home.

As Mindi was standing in the spotlight introducing the concert, he was struck with pride and emotion when the stage light illuminated the front section of the audience. Beaming ear-to-ear, he could clearly see his dad seated next to Rose, Mindi's parents, his brother and sister and their families, along with Mindi's college bestie, Jamie, and of course, Dr. Linda Patel and hundreds of doctors and healers from her organization.

Rich looked out at the pink and blue sunset and over the vast sold-out audience and listened to Mindi's reverberating voice.

"Thank you for joining us on this unforgettable night of music and unity as we come together to raise awareness and support for Healing Vision, an international organization dedicated to healing and restoring eyesight worldwide. All proceeds from the concert will go toward supporting Healing Vision, an organization that is working toward a connected world."

The sold-out crowd roared in response as Mindi ended with…

"Let's Rock-the-Rocks!"

The Concert for Healing Vision had begun.

***

Several hours passed in what seemed like a flash, and as the encore began, Rich was invited to the stage to perform his song with all the artists. It was a moment of personal magic!

While the applause continued, Rich yelled as he and Mindi were rushing backstage to thank the bands.

Mindi, "Listen to the crowd—they haven't let up!"

"It's amazing, isn't it?" Mindi said breathlessly. "I can't believe it's over!"

"Oh, I think it's just the beginning," Rich said, recognizing that this time, it was him leading her backstage, not the other way around.

As they mingled with the bands and the crew, he noticed that Mindi was more animated than he'd ever seen her. Gone was the ever-professional executive producer. This Mindi was happy to join the festivities while they were congratulated by the musicians, crews, and staff that had helped make the concert a resounding success.

It was hours before they had a moment alone.

"The last time we were backstage, it didn't end quite like this," Rich remarked with a smile.

"No, it didn't, but we weren't the same people back then, were we?" she grinned. "It's been a learning process, for sure. And what about you? In your dream of writing a hit song, was this the moment you imagined? I heard them say that there have been so many paid downloads that it briefly crashed the website … imagine the impact of the money raised tonight!"

"So much has changed for both of us," Rich agreed. "It was risky to start all over, and we both know that it took a lot of hard work to make this happen. Do you have any regrets, Mindi?"

"Not at all," she said as she reached out to place both of his hands in hers. "I feel like I've come full circle. *We've* come full circle, too, but this time around, we're in perfect rhythm. This is only the beginning, Rich. I think we're just getting started … in more ways than one."

UNIVERSAL RELATIONSHIP RHYTHMS

In the **Rhythm of Respect**, we show up and we're present, we listen, we build trust, and lead with compassion and authenticity. **When we show Respect, our relationships are collaborative and empowered!**

***

In the **Rhythm of Responsibility**, we are intentional, we are committed, we communicate clearly, and we stand accountable for our actions. **When we are Responsible, expectations are aligned, and our relationships are full of possibilities.**

***

In the **Rhythm of Reframing** we lead with gratitude, we accept the traumas of our past without letting them limit us, we meet people where they are, and honor feedback as neutral. **When we Reframe, a new perspective emerges, and a shift happens!**

***

In the **Rhythm of Resilience**, we stand up and step forward with consistent action, and accept support to courageously face and navigate inevitable change. **When we are Resilient, our relationships are inspired and renewed!**

AFTERWORD

A MESSAGE FROM THE AUTHORS

Show up with respect, stand up and be responsible,
reframe limiting beliefs, step forward with resilience.

We have one life to live, one body, and one planet.

Relationships are the most significant factor impacting and influencing every aspect of our lives … personal, professional, and with the planet. Like air and water, good or bad, relationships cannot be avoided, and we could not survive without them. Every relationship begins with a connection, and we believe that *mastering connection with universal relationship rhythms is the next evolution in our human story and our life legacy*!

Whether emotional, physical, intellectual, or spiritual, we are in many relationships and connected to someone or something from the time we wake up in the morning. Whether we know all the people around us or not, **we are all connected as humans first, and that's where the bottom line begins.**

We are husband and wife, and we've been living, loving, playing, and working side by side, choosing each other every day for nearly twenty years. For as long as we've been together, people constantly ask, "How do you work together as a couple without making each other crazy and still have a … you know, personal life?" We had never really looked at or dissected our relationship, in fact, we were afraid to. We thought we might break it by analyzing it. We got curious, though, and we wondered if there were commonalities that flow across thriving relationships at work, at home, and beyond. So, we began an expedition of discovery.

While working together globally as executive event producers, business consultants, coaches, authors, and mentors, we've been honored to work with non-profits, corporations, celebrities, Heads of State, and heads of households. From classrooms to boardrooms, and big brands, we began to notice clear distinctions with all successful relationships.

We recognized that all relationships have a beat, a tempo, and a rhythm! Sometimes relationships can be smooth like cool jazz, or driving like rock, rap, or country, all with varied intensity that impact our connections! In our daily lives, our relationships can experience all these rhythms.

Think about your favorite song, movie, play, or book, and how you connect with them from your heart. They are all written about relationships! Global borders, the environment, technology, and human rights are all shared and fought over because of relationships! Valuing the importance of relationships, corporations spend $67 billion annually on Customer Relationship Management systems (CRMs).

As our discovery continued, we identified four universal relationship rhythms: *Respect, Responsibility, Reframing, and Resilience.* Working in unison across our personal, professional, and planetary relationships, these "rhythms" can reduce stress and heart disease and improve the quality of life. Relationships may be the unsung determiner of success and the predictor of healthy living. We see these four universal rhythms as the lifeblood of mastering connection in every aspect of our lives.

Who would you say your most important relationship is with? Your family, friends, your community, or your work? We are talking about all of these relationships.

Each of us comes to our relationships today from a long legacy of relationships from our past, our parents' past, and their parents before them. They paved the way for who we are today and shaped much of what we believe to be true about relationships … with family and friends, with social issues, with our community, with health and wellness, time, and money. We are their living legacy! We inherit our relationships to family, culture, and our faith, and the beliefs of those who raised us. Then, from our youth and into adulthood, we also have the opportunity to "choose" our relationships.

Today we see individuals, corporations, foundations, countries, cities, and states all in desperate need of shifting their mindset regarding the significance of relationships. When we think about where to begin in mastering our relationships, the first place, of course, is by noticing the most significant relationship, 24/7, including while we sleep, is with … ourselves! Think about it, how we feel about ourselves shows up in all our relationships. It is an inside-out job!

Recognizing our connection with everyone, and every living part of our planet, is at a tipping point! We invite you to look at your relationships, personal, professional, and with the planet. Ask yourself, "Am I living in relationship "to," or am I choosing to be in relationship "with" my life and those in it? Am I living in-sync and in tune with the Relationship Rhythms and choosing, *Respect, Responsibility, Reframing, and Resilience?"*

Isn't it time for relationships to move front-and-center on the global stage we call life?

Our choices determine our future, and mastering connection with relationship rhythms is the next evolution in our human story and our life legacy!

Visit www.SegalLeadershipGlobal.com
Follow us on Instagram: _the_rfactor
Scan for a FREE Relationship Rhythm Tool

Connect With Us

EACH OF US

Written By Ken Ashby

Each of us a star, a brilliant light
Every star illuminates the night in its own way
All the lights combine to make the day
Tomorrow is not up to someone else
The hope you have is hope that you can trust
The truth is that the future is up to each of us

Each of us can build, each of us can teach
And reach inside, we can guide
And what we leave is up to each of us

Each of us can stand for something good
Every time we rise, we elevate the place we live
We expand our souls by what we give
Tomorrow is not up to someone else
The hope you have is hope that you can trust
The truth is that the future is up to each of us

Each of us can build, each of us can teach
And reach inside, we can guide
And what we leave is up to each of us

Do we really know or understand
The power we all have in our hand
The answer's beyond a twist of fate
The question's not IF
but WHAT will we create

Each of us can build, each of us can teach
And reach inside, we can guide
And what we leave is up to each of us

ACKNOWLEDGEMENTS

I n so many ways, this book and the journey that has brought us to this point have been a lifetime in the making. We've been fortunate for our global experiences and the amazing relationships that surround us personally and professionally. To those who have contributed so much to enrich our lives, you know who you are, you deeply touch us, and we cherish and hold our friendships dear. We appreciate and are grateful for the abundance that you bring into our lives.

For your wise counsel, support, and collaboration as The *R*Factor was finding its voice...

Dr. Gregory Reid
Patti McKenna
Wesley Bryant

For your mentorship throughout our leadership journey...

**Blanton & Betty Belk, Dave and Brenda Mackay,
David Corbin, Erik Swanson, Forbes Riley,
Ilan and Louisa Bohm, Judith Rich, Lisa Kalmin,
Lynne Sheridan, Michael Strasner, Paul Colwell,
Shanda Sumpter and Ash Gundahari, Sharon Lechter,
Wally McGuire, William E. Gregory, PhD**

For your insights, feedback, and friendship on this book journey...

**Betsy Myers, Cindy Glanzrock, Connie Desaulniers,
Kathi Sharpe-Ross, Keith Kehlbeck and Ali Webb,
Robert Shabkie and Dan Kough, Victor McGuire**

ABOUT THE AUTHORS

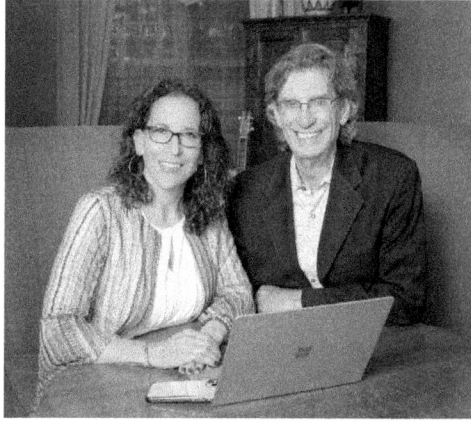

K en Ashby and Maris Segal coach, consult, and collaborate with executives, entrepreneurs, celebrities, and rising leaders to identify and bring their professional, personal, and philanthropic vision to life. Spanning four decades and forty countries, they combine their relationship marketing expertise with head and heart leadership to build meaningful connections and impactful strategies that drive their client's internal and external success.

As "America's Master Connectors," Ken and Maris live by the philosophy that, "We are all connected as humans first, and that's where the bottom line begins."

Together and individually, working across the public and private sectors, they have served a wide spectrum of local and global leaders, consumer and financial brands, causes, and policy makers. This dynamic duo also leverages Ken's international award-winning singer songwriting gifts to develop collaborative teams with a songwriting workshop series. From board rooms and classrooms to Harvard, the White House, and Super Bowl Halftimes, Ken and Maris are also known for uniting diverse populations with innovative cross-cultural marketing and personal development programs that bring a creative voice to issues.

The *RFactor*: Universal Rhythms for Leading Prosperous Relationships sits at the core of their work as certified Executive and Relationship coaches. Ashby and Segal set a path for every client to build high-performing businesses and elevate personal and professional leadership for maximum impact and a 360-degree thriving life! As authors, they have been featured in thirteen Amazon best-selling leadership centered books. They speak regularly and were recently featured at TEDx Farmingdale.

To connect, visit www.SegalLeadershipGlobal.com

Follow Ken Ashby and Maris Segal on Instagram: _the_rfactor